Living Unbroken

"Divorce is a soul-level wound so deep and so profound that it probably seems like there is no hope for your future. If you will let Tracie walk with you on your divorce journey, she will lead you to the only source of healing that can provide you with the hope and peace you so desperately seek."

Steve Grissom, founder,
DivorceCare support groups

"It isn't often that you get to see a friend walk from total devastation to victory, but I've had the privilege. Watching Tracie walk back to the land of living after the heartbreak of divorce was watching God in action. If she can do it, so can you, and *Living Unbroken* is the tool that will pave your way to victory and restoration."

Wendy Pope, author of *Hidden Potential*, founder
and executive director of Word Up Ministries

"Whether you feel like your marriage is unraveling or you're grasping at the sharp, shattered pieces of life after divorce, this book is for you. With transparency and gut-honest truth, Tracie Miles courageously shares her personal story while helping you navigate through your own spousal storm. Like a friend who understands what you're going through and a mentor who offers you renewed hope, Tracie shines a light on all the ways you're not alone. Reading this book will be your best next step to a brighter tomorrow!"

Leah DiPascal, author, Bible teacher, cofounder of *Lighten Up Sweet Pea* podcast

"Nobody ever goes into marriage expecting to divorce, and many don't want it when it happens. *Living Unbroken* is a raw account of Tracie Miles's personal journey to reclaim her life and her heart after her divorce. Tracie shares the real and the raw while pointing you back to truths you, too, can cling to when you find yourself in a similar situation. She acknowledges the pain, grief, shame, loneliness, and guilt all too many will go through but then gives you hope to turn the page and step into the next part of your journey."

Dr. Michelle Bengtson, author of the award-winning book *Breaking Anxiety's Grip*

"As someone who has suffered through the heartbreak and loss of a broken marriage, I found great comfort in every word, on every page of this book. Tracie Miles has been there, and she understands the pain and brokenness that lingers on, long after the divorce is finalized. In *Living Unbroken*, she offers help, healing, hope, guidance, and biblical wisdom so you can live with joy and freedom after divorce."

Courtney Joseph, author, blogger at WomenLivingWell.org and GoodMorningGirls.org

"*Living Unbroken* is an inspirational book not only for those who have endured the pain of a divorce but also for those who have walked or are walking through difficult and unexpectedly painful seasons in their marriage. Writing from her own personal experience, Tracie Miles will help you learn how to heal, thrive, and reclaim your life for Christ while rededicating your heart to Him and His purpose."

Janet Jones Kendall, writer, wife, mother

"Living Unbroken is an excellent resource for anyone who has been heartbroken through the devastation of divorce. I have gone through two divorces, and the last shattered my heart. Tracie knows what that feels like and knows how heartbroken you can feel during and after. I can't truly put into words the feeling you get while reading along with her; she becomes a trusted friend, even though you may have never met her, and you no longer feel alone going through this."

Malinda Koonce, divorce survivor, blogger

Living
Unbroken

Living Unbroken

Reclaiming Your
Life and Your Heart
after Divorce

Tracie Miles

DAVID C COOK

transforming lives together

LIVING UNBROKEN
Published by David C Cook
4050 Lee Vance Drive
Colorado Springs, CO 80918 U.S.A.

Integrity Music Limited, a Division of David C Cook
Brighton, East Sussex BN1 2RE, England

Library of Congress Control Number 2020946264
ISBN 978-0-8307-8095-2
eISBN 978-0-8307-8096-9

© 2021 Tracie Miles
The author is represented by and this book is published in association with the
literary agency of WordServe Literary Group, Ltd., www.wordserveliterary.com.

The Team: Susan McPherson, Alice Crider, Judy Gillispie,
Kayla Fenstermaker, Jon Middel, Susan Murdock
Cover Design: Jon Middel
Cover Photo: Getty Images

Printed in the United States of America
First Edition 2021

1 2 3 4 5 6 7 8 9 10

112020

Contents

Introduction   11

Chapter 1: When Your World Is Shattered   21

Chapter 2: Accepting What Is, What Isn't, and Who You Are   45

Chapter 3: Your Fears Are No Match for God   61

Chapter 4: Overcoming Loneliness   85

Chapter 5: Making the Most of Your Singleness   101

Chapter 6: Breaking the Power of Shame   121

Chapter 7: Releasing the Burden of Guilt   135

Chapter 8: Girl, You Are Not Crazy   155

Chapter 9: Love Conquers All   175

Chapter 10: It's Time to Turn the Page   191

Notes   215

Introduction

You were married; now you're not.

You once had a life partner; now you don't. You thought you'd grow old together; now you wonder if you'll be alone forever. Maybe your husband had an affair and left you. Maybe you had an affair. Maybe he said he didn't love you anymore or told you he was in love with someone else. Or maybe you simply grew apart.

Regardless of how your singleness came to be, you're struggling. Hurting so deeply it feels worse than physical pain. You're drowning in confusion about how your spouse could do this to you and your children, or how you got to this place. You feel more alone than you ever have. The future that once seemed secure now looks terrifying. You don't know who you are anymore. You hate this unfamiliar life you're stuck in. You wonder if you'll ever get over what happened. Will you even survive?

You feel broken and lost, and you long to feel whole and happy again, but happiness may seem impossible right now. Like a thing of the past. You may feel as if nobody understands your pain. Not a person on the planet can comprehend what you're really going through. You may be feeling judged, misunderstood, embarrassed—or disposable, unlovable, not enough, and tossed aside. You might feel like you don't fit in with married couples or singles groups. You likely feel scared and all alone on this unknown path, this journey you never wanted to be on.

Friend, I get it. I've been there too. That is exactly where I found myself almost five years ago.

But I've discovered that in spite of how you may think and feel right now, you can feel whole and happy again. Even though it seems like the life you knew is over—and in some ways it is—life itself is not over. There is so much good in store for you, including happiness.

We do not have to live in brokenness.

After my marriage of more than twenty-five years abruptly ended, months of heartbreak, tears, pain, and fear had taken their toll. Exhaustion settled deep in my bones, a deeper tiredness than multiple nights of sleeplessness could ever cause. It wasn't merely physical fatigue but mental and emotional exhaustion that weakened my desire to even get out of bed in the morning, much less perform any task that required brainpower or seeing other humans.

One morning, as another day dawned and sun streaks began to peek through my bedroom windows, the heavy awareness of an empty bed and an empty house took my breath away. A house in which more than twenty years of life had taken place was now empty—not only because of separation but also because of a newly empty nest. A house that once hustled and bustled with babies and toddlers and the sounds of little feet shuffling around upstairs. A house in which the adventures of raising middle schoolers and teens took place. A house with college kids moving in and out during holidays and summer breaks. A house that used to feel and sound like love, security, and family. Yet now it was painfully void of any life and filled with a deafening silence.

I dragged myself out of bed, put on a warm robe, and walked to the kitchen to start a pot of coffee. As the caffeine brewed, I looked out the back door to my deck, where the morning sun made the dew sparkle. My tired mind was instantly lulled into the past. As if the events were happening right in front of my eyes again, memories came to life.

Crisp spring mornings spent eating Froot Loops cereal on the deck with three little ones excitedly chattering about the day ahead. Family cookouts and laughter during the spring and summer months while we listened to our favorite Jimmy Buffett songs. Countless cold nights huddled as a family in front of the crackling firepit, wrapped in blankets and hugs while eating s'mores. All the birthday parties, pumpkin-carving festivities, gatherings of friends, and graduation celebrations that had taken place on those faded, aging planks of wood.

My eyes began to well up, blurring my view. A tear escaped and trickled down my face as I realized how bittersweet those memories were and how different my reality looked now. A reality I never expected or wanted. A reality I tried so hard to avoid for so many years. But it was the reality I now lived in nonetheless. I always knew the kids would grow up and one day leave my little nest, but I never thought I would be left living in that nest all alone.

Years had flown by, with one daughter working as a teacher, one still in college, and my son a junior in high school. My husband was no longer in the picture, and all contact had ceased. Now, instead of packing lunches and rushing out the door to school, managing sibling spats, cartoons blaring from the television, teens texting and laughing, loud sleepovers, piles of laundry begging to be washed, and dinner simmering on the stove filling the house with delicious aromas, all that was happening each day ... was nothing.

I forced myself to look away from the glass door, pour a cup of coffee, and assume my normal morning position—curled up on the couch, aimlessly staring at the television, wondering how and why I had arrived at this painful place in life where heartbreak, loneliness, and fear were my constant companions. Sometimes my only companions. I pondered how much life had changed, unsure if the pain would ever end and if life would—or could—ever be okay again.

Let's Do This Together

I know firsthand the stress of walking through a struggling marriage that doesn't seem to get better no matter how hard you try. Or at times it seems better, only to have a problem or hurt or betrayal blindside you. Broken promises abounding. Trust being shattered time and time again.

I know the indescribable emotional pain of separating from the person you once committed to spending the rest of your life with— someone you possibly still love and care about. And I understand the unfathomable heartbreak, devastation, trauma, and suffocating fears that strangle the joy from the deepest corner of your soul, making every breath difficult as you come to grips with the fact that separation and divorce have become your reality. A strange, unwanted, lonely, scary life that you never imagined would be *your* life.

I know what it's like to feel so lost and broken that not only do you think you can never put the pieces of your broken life and family back together, but you also believe you can never be whole, healed, or happy again. I've experienced this depth of brokenness, as you likely have, since you're holding this book. But I have good news.

We do not have to live in brokenness. How we live is our choice. Our happiness is up to us, and God has so much goodness in store for us. Life is a gift, and it can be good no matter what we are facing. "How?" you might ask. "Like seriously, how?"

Because we are reassured all throughout the Scriptures that Jesus cares about us. He died to save us, and He lives to heal us and stay by our side.

> Life is a gift, and it can be good no matter what we are facing.

Two of my favorite go-to verses when hopelessness or sadness tries to creep back in are "He heals the brokenhearted and bandages their wounds" (Ps. 147:3) and "The LORD is close to the broken-hearted; he rescues those whose spirits are crushed" (Ps. 34:18). It's comforting to know that even when we feel abandoned, He is still by our side, and even when our hearts are broken and we think we'll never be happy again, we can trust that in His timing He will help us put the pieces of our hearts back together. Joy will come again and, oh, how I wish I could be there to see the look on your face when you realize this is actually possible! I would love to witness the light come on inside your soul, your eyes brighten, and your smile return when renewal, transformation, courage, strength, growth, acceptance, and an unfamiliar sense of contentment and happiness begin to pierce every ounce of who you are. That divine moment when you realize you too can be whole and happy again. I would love to be sitting across the table from you when you feel the sensation of joy slowly seeping through your body like a cup of hot chocolate on a frigid day. As if you could feel the brightness of your future warming your body from the inside out. Imagine it for yourself.

It is possible to be unbroken—to live unbroken, to feel unbroken—despite our circumstances.

My prayer is that this book will help you achieve this incredible feeling, gain a new level of confidence, glean ideas for moving forward, and feel encouraged and equipped to embrace hope and start truly believing happiness and a life you love is within reach. I also hope you will feel less alone in this journey.

Your Heart Can Be Mended

Only Jesus can truly mend broken hearts and handle the problems in our lives. But as you read through these pages, I hope to help you take your first steps toward healing the wound nobody can see and opening the door for Jesus to begin mending the shattered pieces of your heart. Crucial steps toward relieving the pain that right now may seem untreatable. This is the very reason God laid it on my heart to write this book. I have lived out the promise found in Matthew 5:4—"Blessed are those who mourn, for they will be comforted" (NIV)—and I want you to experience this same comfort that only Jesus can provide.

Maybe just as you have been doing, as I worked toward putting my life back together after my divorce, I anxiously searched for books and resources that would speak hope and peace into my exhausted heart, soul, and mind. In my quest to find myself and my happiness again, I just needed something to help me put my feet on the floor each day and get out of bed one more time.

Although many people loved me and would have done anything in the world for me, they grew understandably weary of my sadness and depression after a while. My heart desperately needed and longed for encouraging words from a woman who had been in my shoes, who knew my deepest pain points, who knew what I was feeling and the reassurances I needed to hear. Someone who knew what words of encouragement would lift my spirits and what hopeful promises would shift my heart to a better place. A woman who understood and could help me climb out of this pit, one scraped knee after another, and start putting the fragments of my broken heart and life back together.

I longed to learn from someone who had experienced and survived the intense emotional pain that cut deeper than any physical pain ever could. Someone who could keep me from drowning in my fears and sorrows. Someone who could hold me up when I couldn't hold myself up.

I came across countless books on how to save a marriage, be a better wife, overcome infidelity and unforgiveness, reconcile, and build a better relationship. There were books from experts on the topic of divorce, but most of them seemed to focus mainly on legal matters, child custody, financial planning, and dating again. But that wasn't what my heart needed. I longed for an infusion of hope, peace, and spiritual support. I needed to know how to keep breathing on those days when I had no energy—not mere facts about navigating this new journey legally or financially, although, of course, those are important too.

I just needed a girlfriend to say, "Tracie, I know this is hard, but I promise you will be okay. You will survive and here's how. In fact, in time, you will be better than okay. You will be happy again and thriving. **You've got this. God's got you. Let's do this together.**"

> *It is possible to be unbroken—to live unbroken, to feel unbroken—despite our circumstances.*

However, finding a book with these promises and that type of support, especially one founded on faith, seemed futile. I assumed that was because divorce is not considered a "Christian" topic, which only confounded my feelings of failure, aloneness, and shame-filled brokenness.

Although many of the books I found could have been helpful (and a few were) for navigating all the twists, turns, and learning curves of my new battles, they could not help my spiritual, mental, and emotional state improve. They couldn't lead me to deep healing nor excite me about the scary, unknown future that stretched out ahead of me. I needed a friend who had walked in my shoes to hold my hand and walk alongside me, even if only through words on a page. I never found that friend or book, but I did eventually find healing … and now I want to share what I've learned with you.

I hope you will allow me to be that girlfriend for you. The one who has walked in your shoes. The one who gets you and understands the fears and feelings you're too embarrassed to share. The one who knows just what you need to hear to get through another day. The one who can help you reclaim your faith in yourself and in God.

I am by no means on the other side of this battle. I still have a long way to go toward where I want to be. But I can say I am not where I was a little less than five years ago when my world imploded, and I am thankful for and proud of that. I am grateful God has brought me this far, and I've become a true believer that imperfect progress is better than no progress. Even though I wish my marriage story had turned out differently, I believe God has good plans for me. That truth helps me to continue taking life one day at a time. I've learned that even on those days when it feels as if I'm merely surviving, I am still making it.

In some ways these past several years seem to have dragged by with agonizing slowness, but in other ways it feels as if my journey began just yesterday. I am still so close to the tragedy of being thrust overnight into a world of singleness, single parenthood, and full financial independence, yet far enough down the road to experience the reality that I do not have to live as a broken woman—and life can indeed be good.

I can be as happy as I choose to be, and so can you. I can be content with living alone, and so can you. I can love my life and love those in it, and so can you. I can forgive the unforgivable without bringing that person who hurt me back into my life. I can still have purpose and value. I can feel beautiful, regardless of what others think. I can know who I am. I can be whole.

I don't have to live as a broken woman just because someone's poor choices broke my heart and broke the life I knew. Nor do you. I have chosen to embrace the life I am living. I try to live each day to the fullest, even if it's not the life I thought I would have or the life

I wanted. And, sweet friend, that is what I want for you more than anything.

This journey isn't easy, but it does get easier.

I have so many encouraging things to share with you in the coming chapters, and I hope wherever you are in your journey, this book will help you begin to look forward to starting over. My prayer is for your heart to be so much lighter when you get to the last page. I promise, you will be changed. You will be happier. You will love yourself more and love your life more. You will be relieved and encouraged to leave the pain in the past, pick yourself up one day at a time, and start truly living the life God has you in. You will have a new sense of hope and possibility. And most importantly, you will realize you are not alone.

Though I have not arrived on the shore of victory yet, I'd love to be the friend who can hold your hand and travel there with you. Courage comes from being encouraged. This journey isn't easy, but it does get easier, and you may find you come out even stronger and happier on the other side.

We can live unbroken as we walk into the future with newfound confidence, hope, and joy. You are in charge of your own healing, but we could all use some company along the way. Are you ready to move forward? Let's do this together.

Chapter 1

When Your World Is Shattered

I was with him nearly thirty years. Four of those as a college girl-friend, twenty-five and a half as a wife. On the outside, it looked like we had the perfect life. Beautiful home. Nice cars. Awesome kids, active in sports and excelling in academics. Gorgeous family photos. Great friends. Fun vacations. Special holiday gatherings. But photos and social media feeds can be deceiving. You never know the pain behind someone's smile—until you do.

One day all the turmoil, secrets, and lies that had been causing problems in our marriage erupted like a volcano spewing lava that had been boiling under the surface for decades. Everything was finally out in the open. Proof was in hand. No excuses would suffice. Trust had been broken. Vows had been discarded. Arguments ensued. Tears flowed. Our marriage was instantly broken beyond repair.

My face flushed and my heart disintegrated as my sobbing body collapsed to the floor under the weight of the wrecking ball that had just hit my life. Within a matter of moments, my world was shattered. Never to be the same again. Nor would I be.

That horrible, painful, and unforgettable day marked the first day of a journey I never wanted to embark on. A journey that may look a lot like the one you are now walking. On that day and many days to follow, I needed someone—anyone—to understand what I was going through.

I am fortunate and blessed to have so many friends and family members who have been there to support and encourage me from the moment my husband walked away to the present day. But, although everyone empathized and many shed tears for my children and me, few could truly relate to the loss I was feeling and my sorrow over the death of my marriage.

And that's exactly what divorce is. A death.

The death of a relationship. The death of an intact family. The death of the life you knew. The death of certain friendships. The death of relationships with beloved in-laws. The death of security. The death of dreams. The death of a future.

> Although divorce is the death of a life we once knew, it is not the death of who we are or who we can be.

Divorce evokes intense mourning over the loss of someone who didn't die but instead is still living life—without you. And maybe he seems to be happy, living a great life without a care in the world, maybe even living his best life—without you—and maybe even with someone new.

Yet, it is the type of death people don't share as much sympathy for because there is no funeral to lament the loss. There are no big gatherings of friends and family where everyone brings a casserole or sends flowers, no sympathetic Hallmark cards in the mail, no lengthy posts on Facebook about how much that person will be missed, no closure. Divorce is the type of death that can make you feel more isolated than being on a deserted island. It is a death that is haunting and devastating and penetrates our hearts to the core.

The journey to accepting and recovering from the actual death of a loved one is excruciatingly long and difficult, and the journey to accepting and recovering from separation and divorce is just as difficult and painful. In fact, to lose someone you love because of death is hard enough, but losing someone you love because that person chose to leave you behind is even more heart wrenching. Even if you played a role in the end of your marriage or the divorce was not necessarily your spouse's fault but yours, the end of a marriage can still feel like a death. Change is hard no matter what the circumstances.

Not everyone realizes this or thinks this way, but I do. And my heart breaks knowing you likely do too. The old cliché that tells us not to judge someone until we've walked a mile in that person's shoes is so true. We can never fully comprehend someone's plight until we are in the same plight, so I understand that not everyone could understand. I had never fully understood this level of devastation until I experienced it firsthand.

But I now know what it's like to mourn the living. I know what it's like to be abandoned and wonder if life could ever feel good again. If I could ever feel good about myself again. If I would ever believe I'm enough. If anyone else would ever want me. If I would ever want anyone else. If I could ever trust someone enough to open my heart to love again. If I would even survive.

These are all valid feelings and questions everyone deals with when facing divorce regardless of how many years that marriage existed or what circumstances destroyed it. Actually, even if you knew the end of your marriage was the best decision for you because of continued patterns of infidelity, dishonesty, addiction, abuse, lovelessness, or neglect, the end of a marriage is still beyond painful and hard, and a flood of emotions and fears ensues.

I take comfort in knowing that David in the Bible understood this type of grief. Although he wasn't enduring the exact scenario of separation and divorce, his emotions and pleas to God were the same as someone who is. He wrote, "I am worn out from sobbing. All night I flood my bed with weeping, drenching it with my tears. My vision is blurred by grief; my eyes are worn out because of all my enemies" (Ps. 6:6–7). Sound familiar? It sure does to me.

Until this situation happened in my life, I didn't even know the eyes could produce as many tears as I cried for months and months on end. I discovered what it meant to be emotionally unstable and to live every minute in an on-your-knees desperation for any type of relief from the hurt. I walked out how David was feeling for many, many months—worn out from weeping, lying on pillows wet with tears, waking with bloodshot eyes, and just flat spent.

You see, divorce brings a suffocating grief that all too often goes unacknowledged by others, but it is a deep, aching grief nonetheless. Maybe you've never had anyone share that perspective, and hearing it from me somehow makes you feel a little better.

A Necessary Season

Grief is a painful season to endure, but it is necessary for the healing process to play out. I once read a quote from English poet and hymnodist William Cowper who said, "Grief is itself a medicine."[1] It cleanses our souls from anguish and is the process God can use to help us arrive at a place of healing and wholeness.

Grief is natural and necessary.

The Psalms are filled with hope and reassurance for every stage of life, but there are two verses in particular that are critical to remember as we walk this journey of grief together, whether you are enduring the beginning of a separation or living in the aftermath of divorce. I shared these in the introduction, but they are worth mentioning again. The first is Psalm 34:18, one of the most reassuring verses in the Bible when it comes to grief in any form: "The LORD is close to the brokenhearted; he rescues those whose spirits are crushed." The Lord is with you, my friend. He is closer than you think. He is who will hold you tight during your season of grief. The second is Psalm 147:3: "He heals the brokenhearted and bandages their wounds."

Let these sweet verses give you hope. God will not only hold you close but, in time, He will also rescue you from your grief and heal your heart. This is His promise to you. He is a God who heals hearts, minds, bodies, and lives. Sometimes immediately and sometimes over time through a process of growth and learning. It's not a question of *if* He will heal you and bandage your wounds but *when*.

Rest assured, better days are coming. Put your hope in Jesus and let it stay there. As Psalm 39:7 says, "So, Lord, where do I put my hope? My only hope is in you." Tuck that verse in your heart as well, and let these be ones you hold on to as we walk this path.

Grief is natural and necessary. I believe the first step to recovering from such deep grief is acknowledging what it is and letting yourself experience it without shame. Knowing this, let's take one chapter to acknowledge and deal with our grief before we step onto this progressive path of finding our smiles again.

The Stages of Grief

It's been said there are five stages of grief when someone we love dies: denial, anger, bargaining, depression, and acceptance.[2] The same stages apply when we're grieving the loss of a spouse who didn't die but is no longer a part of our life. When we're mourning the loss of dreams and plans, an unbroken family, a father to our children, the comfort of home, in-laws, friends, financial security, and more. We may grieve who our spouse once was and who we were as a couple. We may even grieve the loss of the person we once were. We may grieve the loss of happiness that has been replaced with a heaviness and a sadness we can't seem to shake. In fact, it might even seem we're grieving the death of everything we once knew.

The question is not whether you will go through this five-stage grief process but how you will go through it and how long you will take to navigate each stage. In fact, it's important to realize that since we are emotional creatures and the grief process is difficult, we will likely all swing back and forth through the five stages of grief as we progress in our healing journeys. We also may not experience the stages in sequential order and will never experience them exactly like someone else.

There will be days when you feel like every time you take two steps forward, you fall three steps back, which is okay and completely normal. This path is hard. No one should expect you to suddenly be "over it," so don't hold yourself to that unattainable standard either. The better you allow yourself to experience each of these stages, understanding that your feelings are normal and valid, the sooner you will begin to get on with your life and discover the happiness waiting for you.

Regardless of how long it takes or the pebbles you trip over on the road to healing, never lose sight of the fact that time heals all wounds. Our hearts will always have scars, but the pain will be less and less as time goes by. Knowing the stages of grief can help you walk out this journey with grace. It's critical to remember that although divorce is the death of a life we once knew, it is not the death of who we are or who we can be. As I've already said, the day will come when you will feel happy and whole again. Free to start a new life. Free to be who you want to be and excited about who you are and what lies ahead. I promise that time will come, and this book can help you get there.

Stage 1: Denial
Avoidance, Confusion, Elation, Shock, Fear

Typically, one of the first things we experience when a marriage ends is absolute shock—especially if it ended abruptly and unexpectedly due to an affair, pornography, addiction, or abuse, or because your spouse said he was no longer in love with you.

In the first few months of being separated from my husband, I was in shock and denial. My mind was poisoned daily with negative thoughts about myself. *Why did this happen? What did I do wrong? Why wasn't I enough? What's wrong with me?* I couldn't think straight or concentrate on anything. I felt like a robot going through the motions of each day with a freight train resting on my chest.

I struggled to accept that this was the end of our marriage, and I grappled with all the reasons it had ended, most of which were beyond my control. I tried to deny the reality of what had happened that forever altered my future, leaving me clinging to an empty hope that maybe everything would miraculously change. Maybe I would wake up from this nightmare and it would all be over. Maybe my husband's heart would change. Maybe he would choose me, our kids, and our life and we would end up okay. Maybe I could forgive and try to forget and move on.

But in my heart I knew none of that would happen nor could it happen because of all the circumstances at hand. Although my heart wished differently, deep down I knew reconciliation was not possible because of a historical pattern of certain behaviors, so the denial stage didn't last as long for me as it might for others. But it still took many, many months to get through.

As we progress through this chapter, you might find yourself trying to read these words through tears because what I'm describing sounds all too painfully familiar. You may feel pulled back into hard memories of your own situation, reliving those terrible times in your head. But that is not my intent, sweet friend. I want you to understand we are sisters, we get each other, and we are on this journey toward healing together. And I want you to know you'll get through this because millions of women and men go through it— and survive. Grief is confusing and hard, but eventually we will make it to the other side of the pain.

Look for the Positives

Even though it's hard to imagine when we're in the midst of grief, some benefits are tucked within each of these five stages. Each phase serves a beneficial purpose and propels you into the next, steering you closer to where you want to be—recovered, healed, whole, and embracing your new life with joy.

It's important to know that the stage of denial isn't necessarily a bad thing because it helps us handle the initial realization that the marriage is over. Shock and denial cushion our hearts against trying to deal with all the pain at once. Sometimes the details are too sharp to swallow. Sometimes the loss is too big to understand or fully embrace and we need to allow ourselves time to deal with reality. Denying what's happened or what we fear might happen helps us keep emotions in check rather than becoming completely overwhelmed and paralyzed with grief and fear. It helps keep the freak-out moments to a minimum, at least for a while, and gives our brains time to adjust to the loss.

I learned that if I tried to process every aspect of my life that had changed and tried to figure everything out that needed to be figured out all at once, anxiety would grip my soul like a tourniquet. Our hearts and minds can only handle so much, so taking things slowly during this denial stage allows the healing process to begin. Nobody wants to accept the unacceptable or believe the unbelievable. So give yourself all the time you need with a huge dose of grace and patience.

Stage 2: Anger
Frustration, Irritation, Anxiety

For at least six months after our separation, I continued to falsely think that maybe, just maybe, some miracle would happen and we could salvage our marriage. Even though our relationship had been on the rocks for quite some time, I still loved my husband and wanted our family to stay together. I held out hope that my prayers for a solid marriage and a devoted, loving husband would be answered. I pleaded with God to work miracles I knew only He could do.

But as more time passed and my husband continued with the same lifestyle choices and relationships that had torn our marriage apart despite countless promises to change, I became frustrated, confused, and angry. I experienced levels of anger I didn't even know existed.

A mixture of hurt, resentment, embarrassment, and disbelief heightened my anger each day. My mental battle raged, and questions fueled my pain-laced bitterness. *How could he do this to me? How could he hurt me this way? How could he throw away the beautiful life we built and the family we created together? How could he betray me like this? How could he lie to me week after week and not feel any remorse? How could I be so naive? Why doesn't he want to spend time with our children? How could he not love them enough to love their mother? How could he just walk away from our life?* Anger ran rampant—and not just at him.

I was also angry at life. *Why me? How is this fair? What did I do to deserve this? Why do other people have happy marriages and I wasn't blessed with that? Why does everyone else seem to be so in love, celebrating milestone anniversaries all over social media, and my own husband can't even love me?*

I was angry at myself. *Why did I stay in this difficult marriage this long, only to have it blow up anyway? Why did I not stand firm years ago and have enough courage and strength to refuse to tolerate and enable trust-robbing behaviors? Why did I allow myself to be treated like I didn't matter for so long, leaving me feeling like I had little to no value? What is wrong with me? Why was I never enough?*

And you know what? I have to admit I was also angry at God. My prayers were filled with questions. *Why would You allow this to happen to us, God? How many years have I prayed for my marriage—all prayers You seemed to ignore? Why wouldn't You want my marriage to succeed if the marriage covenant is so important in Your eyes? Why didn't You protect and preserve our family? Why would You let my children suffer with this pain? Why do I have to be so alone?*

Angry pity party for one, please.

I'm not saying it's right to be mad at God, but it is all right. He already knows our thoughts, as we're told in Psalm 139:4: "You know what I am going to say even before I say it, LORD." We can be real with Him. We don't need to act religious and try to hide our anger or assume that as Christians we shouldn't get angry at God, because not only can He handle our anger but He also understands and has compassion for us regardless.

I was angry. Infuriated. Offended. Outraged. Fuming. You get the picture. And it's not pretty.

Truthfully, I had every right to be angry. I had been hurt, betrayed, and treated wrongly. And if you've gone through a similar situation or even if your circumstances are different from mine, it's likely you are angry too. And it is okay, friend. Christians are human, and anger is a natural response to injustice, betrayal, dishonesty, or mean-spiritedness.

It is normal and actually necessary to feel angry and deal with our anger. Suppressing or denying our emotions is not healthy, and they will eventually reach a boiling point if not acknowledged and dealt with. An article about the five stages of grief said this about anger:

> When you experience a grief event, you might feel disconnected from reality—that you have no grounding anymore. Your life has shattered and there's nothing solid to hold onto. Think of anger as a strength to bind you to reality.... The direction of anger toward something or somebody is what might bridge you back to reality and connect you to people again. It is a "thing." It's something to grasp onto—a natural step in healing.[3]

Anger was definitely a "thing" for me. Day after day, the feeling of righteous anger would overpower my heart's desire to forgive. Although I would ask God for the ability to grant mercy and forgiveness to my husband, for my own peace if nothing else, my long mental list of justifications for being angry would override my hollow prayer. Plus, every time I tried to forgive and offer love, something else would happen to make me feel hurt or betrayed, and my heart would get twisted up all over again.

It was as if voices in my head were arguing with each other, with one trying to convince me I was justified in feeling angry and the other trying to convince me forgiveness and mercy were the best choice. But it's hard to forgive when the one who has done the hurting refuses to repent, which left me constantly thinking, *I have a right to be angry. Anyone would agree.* That's why James 1:19 was not a piece of Scripture I wanted to read during this time, yet God continually brought it to my mind: "My dear brothers and sisters, take note of this: Everyone should be quick to listen, slow to speak, and slow to become angry" (NIV).

This verse is hard to digest when you've been betrayed and rejected and your heart is broken. It's not what you want to hear when your trust in someone has been violated and your entire future has been altered as a result. Forgiveness doesn't come easily when you're deeply hurt. But it can come eventually.

Notice how the verse above says "everyone" should be slow to speak and slow to anger, leaving no room for excuses or righteous indignation from those who know they have been wronged. James was imploring God's people to understand the damage that negative thoughts and emotions can cause in our hearts. He knew unforgiveness doesn't change an offender's life; it changes ours. It doesn't change the other person's heart; it changes ours. It doesn't change that person's ability to live and love life, but it does change ours.

> *Forgiveness doesn't come easily when you're deeply hurt. But it can come eventually.*

From a worldly perspective, I *did* have every right to be angry and unforgiving, as you might as well. But from a godly perspective, my anger and unforgiveness were holding me hostage to unhappiness. The longer I felt justified in holding on to my anger, the stronger the foothold the devil had in my heart and the tighter the chains became. I wanted to be free, even if it meant forgiving someone who I felt didn't deserve my forgiveness.

As I continued reading, James 1:22 stood out to me: "Do not merely listen to the word, and so deceive yourselves. Do what it says" (NIV). God softened my heart with this passage, making me aware that although I had forgiven my husband with my words and tried to have compassion for him, I had not truly forgiven with my heart. Forgiveness empowered me to stop letting someone who didn't care about me control my mind and emotions.

Anger and unforgiveness are buddies that gang up on our hearts. But forgiveness releases us from the damage they can cause. Forgiveness doesn't condone or accept other people's behavior, nor does it mean we have to allow those people back into our lives, but it does help us open the door to our own happiness. And as Christians, we can always choose to seek God's help in dealing with our anger regardless of who or what it is directed to.

One benefit of the anger stage is that you'll feel energized and motivated to keep going and do whatever needs to be done, even on the hardest of days, especially when all your obligations seem overwhelming. It's important not to lash out at your spouse or do anything vengeful, rash, or violent, of course, but letting yourself be angry is an important part of the healing process.

Stage 3: Bargaining
Struggling to Find Meaning, Reaching Out to Others, Telling One's Story

One of the hardest parts of separation or divorce is feeling overwhelmingly helpless and vulnerable. When it seems like everything is out of control, we may find ourselves doing some serious bargaining.

This stage is when we tend to have a lot of conversations with ourselves. We question, *Had we done things differently, would the outcome have been different?* Our thoughts engage in a tug of war as we struggle with all the what-ifs and wonder if there is something we could still do to fix the situation we now find ourselves in. *What if I had been prettier, thinner, younger, a better cook or housekeeper, a better lover? What if I had not nagged him about snoring, staying out too late with buddies after golfing, or not spending enough time with the kids? What if I try to change certain things about myself right now to make things better? Then will we be okay?* My what-if list could go on for days, and I'm sure you have your list of what-ifs as well that could easily slip off your tongue. We all do.

We may bargain with our spouse once separation happens, promising to change in some way or asking him to change and convincing ourselves that he will, all to save the marriage even if it's not good for us in the long run. I found myself doing that for a while; maybe you have done that too.

We may also try to bargain with God, promising that if He'll just fix our problems, change our spouse, or save our marriage, we'll commit to worshipping more, reading our Bible, heading up that church committee, or serving others in selfless ways. We'll promise to stop a bad habit, go on the mission field, do something we feel He's been calling us to do but seemed out of our comfort zone, or simply be more faithful to His Word. We try to think of what we could do that might please God and compel Him to pour favor on us, and we talk to Him as if He doesn't know our true motives.

The problem with bargaining is we might make promises we can't keep because those promises are often fueled by irrational desperation, sadness, and hopelessness. All we want to do is regain control over our circumstances and feel secure, safe, and loved again, so we try to think of what it would take to negotiate with God or others in order to get what we think we want or need.

The real benefits of bargaining come into play if reconciliation is possible. That was not a possibility in my case, but many marriages are saved in this stage when both spouses truly want to work things out. If both are willing to make changes as needed, go to counseling, and put in the hard work, there is a stronger chance of reconciling. However, we have to be careful not to hold on so tightly to false hopes and bargaining tactics that we lose sight of who we are and what's best for us and our lives. Sometimes God removes people from our lives, knowing He has better things in store for us. So it takes a lot of prayer for discernment and guidance to figure out how to navigate this stage.

Bargaining will take place when our emotions are all over the map, our thoughts are shooting in every direction, our minds are trying to make sense of the unthinkable, we can't figure out what to do next, and we're scared. But bargaining is not likely to get us the results we really want. And the weight of this stage of grief can make you think you're going straight-up crazy.

There were many times in the early stages of my marriage breakup that I thought I *was* losing my mind—and it was scary. I could be laughing one moment and break into an epic meltdown the next. I would try hard to focus on doing something and then get so distracted I couldn't get anything done. I felt forgetful, dazed, and confused all the time. Anxiety levels were off the chart, which made it hard to focus on anything. Once, I even passed my exit on the interstate and didn't realize it for thirty minutes because of the haze clouding my thoughts. I would go to a room to get something and forget what I was doing, and my kids would have to tell me things over and over before the information finally stuck. I couldn't seem to stop obsessing about what had happened and feeling buried in worry about all the unknowns. I kept trying to figure out how to fix everything, so I bargained with God, my husband, and myself, all to no avail, which gradually led me to the next stage of grief.

Stage 4: Depression
Overwhelmed, Helpless, Hostile, Wanting to Flee

Deep into this painful journey, I found myself sinking into depression. I was emotionally drained and mentally overwhelmed by the magnitude of problems I was facing. Crying, often unconsolably, was an everyday occurrence. Sometimes multiple times a day. The smallest trigger could send me into an emotional tailspin. My poor children became constant witnesses to my emotional instability, which broke their hearts and in turn broke mine even further. But I was tired to the deepest depths of my soul. I felt helpless to manage my reality. I felt hopeless about my future, and I wanted to run away from the wake of destruction I was living in. But as a mother of three trying to hold my family together and keep a roof over our heads, I had no choice but to fight instead of take flight.

I finally went to the doctor for antidepressants. I also needed an inhaler after being diagnosed with stress-induced asthma. But as the months passed, the time eventually came when I felt I could maybe wean myself off these things. I felt stronger and more confident in my journey, but that time frame will be different for everyone.

Antidepressants or other forms of medication can be a lifesaver for many. I encourage anyone who needs help coping with life to seek out a doctor's advice as well as consult professional Christian counselors. Although finances prevented me from having too many visits with counselors, the few I did have did my heart good. Talking out our problems in a safe place and letting someone speak into our deepest hurts can be the best gift we ever give ourselves. Don't be too proud to seek help when you need it. If you can't afford counseling, find a trusted friend or pastor and push past the fear of being transparent. We all need help from time to time no matter how strong we think we are. Sharing from the heart is good for the soul.

As I moved forward, I poured all my energy into my faith. Praying daily. Reading God's Word. Writing even when I didn't feel like it. Journaling. Reading encouraging books. Trying to think positive thoughts and control my woe-is-me, doom-and-gloom thought patterns.

> We all need help from time to time no matter how strong we think we are. Sharing from the heart is good for the soul.

In the midst of this hurricane I couldn't escape, I had to write a new book—*Unsinkable Faith: God-Filled Strategies to Transform the Way You Think, Feel, and Live*. I had received the book contract a few months prior to the abrupt separation from my husband, and although my life was in shambles, the looming publishing deadline remained.

At first I thought it would be impossible to write that book, considering the circumstances of my life and my unstable mental and emotional state. Who wants to write about learning to live a life of positive thinking when everything in life seems negative? Without God it *would* have been impossible. But God always has a purpose for what we're going through and can do beyond what we can imagine.

It was no surprise to Him that I had to write an uplifting, encouraging, optimism-focused book in the most painful season of my life, and His plan was good. The foundational verse for *Unsinkable Faith*? Hebrews 6:19: "This hope is a strong and trustworthy anchor for our souls." Anchoring my hope in Him is what kept me afloat, especially on those days when I was losing my grip and drowning in my problems and tears.

No matter how difficult it was to keep writing and honor my commitment to my publishing deadline, I now realize writing that book is what kept me sane and helped me truly begin to heal. I studied God's Word every day, researched the power of positive thinking, and focused on practicing what I was writing about, which was capturing and reshaping thought patterns, learning how to live a life of positive thinking, clinging to joy, and trusting God for the future. I was writing about His goodness, even on those days when I doubted it. I uncovered incredible scientific facts about the physical and mental implications that habitual negative thinking has on our bodies and hearts, which in turn helped me be more aware of my own mental, emotional, and physical health. My faith soared when I realized how much science supported exactly what Scripture says about the importance of taking our thoughts captive: "We demolish arguments and every pretension that sets itself up against the knowledge of God, and we take captive every thought to make it obedient to Christ" (2 Cor. 10:5 NIV).

Writing that book changed my mind, then my heart, then my life. I stopped letting my thoughts run my life and chose to try to think positive even in the midst of negative circumstances and to depend on God's peace to get me through. I realized that living in a perpetual pity party was not doing me or my children any good. In fact, in God's perfect timing, I came across this devotional in *Jesus Calling*, which opened my eyes to the damage I was doing to myself. It reminded me of God's sovereign power to help us get through the most difficult of times.

> Self-pity is a slimy, bottomless pit. Once you fall
> in, you tend to go deeper and deeper into the mire.
> As you slide down those slippery walls, you are
> well on your way to depression, and the darkness
> is profound.
>
> Your only hope is to look up and see the Light
> of My Presence shining down on you. Though the
> Light looks dim from your perspective, deep in
> the pit, those rays of hope can reach you at any
> depth.... Psalm 40:2–3[4] ✳

I no longer wanted to be stuck in a pit of sadness and self-pity,
so I began looking for the rays of hope each day even when storm
clouds threatened to block my view. Transformation didn't happen
overnight. In fact, it took nearly two years for me to stop waking
up every day with a feeling of dread and sadness. Pulling out of
depression seemed like a long journey, but it did happen. And it can
happen for you too.

If you're feeling anxious or depressed, invest in yourself by
seeking out the best ways to cope until you can handle things
better. Lean on friends and family like never before, and don't be
too proud to let people know what you're going through and what
you need most. Accept their offers of help. Then allow yourself to
believe there is a light at the end of the tunnel and that overcoming your grief and your fears—and actually enjoying life again—is
right around the bend. With Jesus by your side, you will not stay
in the pit forever.

God always has a purpose for what we're going through and can do beyond what we can imagine.

Nobody wants to feel depressed, but it's a stage most of us will endure in our grief journey. It would be abnormal not to feel intense, heavy sadness at times. If depression is not something you've dealt with in the past, it may be hard to recognize or understand how you are feeling. Or maybe your depression feels so heavy, you find yourself wondering if it would be easier if you just didn't wake up tomorrow. These are critically dangerous thoughts and should be a red flag signifying you need to seek professional or pastoral counseling immediately, surround yourself with friends and family, take care of yourself, and start changing your thought patterns. These thoughts might be a sign that medication is needed for a while to help you cope. Don't ignore these warning signs, and don't be embarrassed to seek help and support. Allow yourself to be sad, but stay acutely aware of your thoughts and where they are taking you. **Remember, your life is still worth living, you are a woman of great worth in God's eyes, and you are loved by many.**

Dealing with sadness and your current reality is healthy and necessary for equipping you to accept what has happened and to learn to deal with it. As sadness subsides, acceptance opens the door for you to stop thinking about what no longer is and start thinking about how to move forward. In the next chapter, I'll show you how acceptance can help you discover how to enjoy the life you now have and feel happy and whole again.

Happiness Prompters

- Look outside your window and find something beautiful to gaze on. Thank God for that little blessing in your day. If you're up to it, look for many blessings and let a smile cross your face each time you see one.

- Treat yourself to something special today. What do you enjoy doing? What makes you feel pampered and refreshed? Choose something and do it.

Healing Steps

1. What stage of grief do you feel you're in today? Write out a summary of where you are now and how you feel you've progressed or stayed stuck in a particular stage. Think about benefits you could experience by trying to move on to the next stage and progress in your healing.

2. List any obstacles preventing you from moving forward, and pray about how to overcome them. Acknowledging what is standing in the way of your happiness is a key factor in overcoming grief.

3. If you haven't already, start a journal either on your computer or in a handheld notebook. Each time you are feeling overwhelmed

with grief, record your thoughts and feelings, prayers, important Scripture verses or devotions you read, and evidence of God working in your life. Include the date for each journal entry.

Caring for You

Do some online research about the stages of grief after divorce. This will help you not only to understand the grieving process better but also to understand you are not alone—and not weird or weak or crazy for feeling the way you do. Search for stories of other women who have gone through these stages already and are now thriving and enjoying their lives. Let their stories give you hope and comfort.

Chapter 2

Accepting What Is, What Isn't, and Who You Are

It takes time, energy, and emotion to walk through all the stages of grief, but the stage of acceptance is eye opening and life changing. We begin to see things with a new perspective, and little sprouts of new life and hope begin to peek out inside us. This is when your new life—and the new you—can truly begin to blossom.

Stage 5: Acceptance ✳
Exploring Options, New Plan in Place, Moving On

Even knowing all the reasons my marriage ended were valid, I still had a hard time accepting it was over. The feelings of grief may have lessened over time, but the sadness over the loss of dreams remained. I didn't want to be alone. I didn't want to be single. I didn't want to be afraid and uncertain about the future, regardless of how deeply I had been betrayed and wounded. Even though I knew reconciliation would have been at the expense of my own self-confidence, self-worth, happiness, and peace, it was hard to envision my future different from what I thought it would be. I was mourning the future I wanted more than the future that actually would have been my reality.

But the time came when I had to accept what wasn't reality and what was. Like it or not, I knew the marriage could not be saved. After about a year with little to no contact, I finally accepted what was true. I had to make the hardest of decisions and figure out how to move on with my life because living in limbo was torture. Sometimes we have to do what is best for ourselves and our lives, not just what we think might be best for others. We have to follow our hearts or risk spending the rest of our lives wishing we had. We also have to accept the fact that when we finally give up on someone or some relationship, it's not because we just don't care anymore or didn't give it our best but because we realize we deserve to be happy and we are worthy of being loved.

Since money was tight, I signed up for a free class at my local library to learn how to file for divorce without a lawyer—a much cheaper version of the process. In the following weeks, I worked through all the tedious legal protocol, and I showed up at the court-house on the assigned day for the divorce court proceeding. I sat anxiously in the courtroom bench with knots in my stomach, my sweet daughter gently holding my hand and my heart. My name was called, a few questions were asked, and then the judge quickly granted the divorce. Twenty-six years down the drain with the sound of a pounding gavel.

I'm not saying it wasn't scary or that I didn't wish things could have turned out differently. I'm not saying it wasn't hard to be the one to actually file for the divorce, all the while wondering whether I was doing the wrong thing or letting God or others down. Divorce is an emotional process as well as a legal process. But accepting what was and letting go of what can't be releases our hearts to focus on what is. Deep in my heart, even though it made me incredibly sad for myself and my children, I knew I had done the right thing, and God had given me peace about it as well. For the first time, I determined to look ahead through the clear lens of hope instead of focusing on the stained rearview mirror of my life.

> Accepting what was and letting go of what can't be releases our hearts to focus on what is.

Accepting the divorce is a critical step in the recovery and healing process. We can spend forever mourning the loss of what could have been, or we can move on with life and choose to enjoy it no matter what. We can be intentional about being grateful for the blessings we do have and stop obsessing over the ones we lost. We can choose to pour our love into the people who *are* in our lives rather than wasting it on ones who chose not to be. We can choose to stop blaming, resenting, and regretting—and start living with joy. When we do, life begins to look different. And it's a great kind of different.

The benefit of acceptance is probably obvious. It doesn't mean you feel off-the-charts happy every day or that you have forgotten the past, alleviated all your fears, and dealt with all your problems. It's not a stage in which life is suddenly perfect. Acceptance simply means you acknowledge what happened but also acknowledge you will make it through with resilience, strength, and faith. It's about embracing your readiness to move forward and start a new life. You begin to believe you will survive after all, and you kick-start a wonderful new life for yourself and your family, knowing, without a shadow of a doubt, that you will actually be okay.

We are all different, and healing takes time. No matter how you progress through the stages, never doubt you are going to make it through. And remember, **God never puts a timetable or a formula on our grief.**

It's okay to not be okay right now. Allow yourself all the time, space, and leniency you need to grieve and to grow closer to the acceptance stage.

You Are Still You

All too often after divorce rips a couple apart, two unfortunate things happen.

One, we often forget our identity in Christ. We've possibly been treated so poorly for so long by our spouse that our self-confidence, self-worth, self-respect, and self-esteem are at an all-time low. Or the divorce itself came out of nowhere and left us reeling, crumbling under the shock, and feeling as if we have no redeemable qualities.

Two, we also often forget who we are as individuals—people divinely created by God with good hearts, beauty inside and out, talents, value, and purpose. Maybe we gave up who we wanted to be because we were always trying to be the person our spouse wanted us to be instead. Maybe the demands of raising children left no time to do the things we really enjoyed.

It's okay to not be okay right now.

I struggled with both of these things a few months into my new normal. Over the many years of struggles, I had forgotten who I was and felt as if I had no value at all. Now facing divorce, I felt lost, alone, and confused about who I was. I became acutely aware of this when the time came for an annual doctor's checkup.

The day of the appointment, I arrived at the doctor's office, checked in at the front desk, then sat down to update the standard forms. Address correct? Check. Age correct? Check. Medical history accurate? Check. Marital status? Stare at wall.

Two little words stumped me completely. As I sat there in a cold waiting room with other patients filling out their forms with ease, tears began to well up in my eyes. I had been thrust into a life of total confusion, chaos, and pain, and I now had no clue how to answer this seemingly simple question.

Was I single? No. Was I married? On paper, yes, but the honest answer was no, at least not in the normal sense of the word. Was I divorced? No. Was I widowed? No, although it felt like it. I was none of the options. So … who was I?

A new moan of emptiness echoed in the caverns of my soul. As I held the incomplete forms, I was faced with the reality that I honestly didn't know who I was anymore. Insecurities, years of feeling I wasn't enough, and heartache had wreaked havoc on my self-confidence. The old me was gone, and this shell of me was now merely existing and trying to survive each day. This new me was so broken she hadn't even considered some of the splintered pieces of her life yet. A new me who was now unexpectedly having a full-blown identity crisis in a doctor's office because she didn't fit into any normal societal box.

I thought to myself, *Who am I now? And where* do *I belong? Not just on this medical form, but in society, friendships, church, and life in general? Who am I, if no longer a wife?*

As I drove home in silence after my appointment, I stared blankly at the road ahead of me, still struggling with this question of my identity. Yet suddenly the silence was broken when I heard a gentle yet life-changing whisper in my spirit.

"The end of your marriage is not the end of you."

It was such a startling thought that could have only come from God, as He was the only One who knew my panicked state of uncertainty. He was the only One who knew the depth of my struggle and therefore the only One who could offer the exact reassurance I so desperately needed. These sweet words served as a holy reminder that my identity was not determined by a role, a title, or a box to check on a form. My identity was determined by my heavenly Father. I felt peace filling my soul and took a deep breath for the first time in a long time.

 The end of your marriage is not the end of you.

I was still me, just a new version of me in a new phase of life. I was still a woman God created in His image. A woman God still had a plan and a purpose for, notwithstanding life's disappointments. A woman who still had value, even if someone else couldn't see it. A woman who was still a mother, daughter, sister, friend, Jesus girl, writer, speaker, tennis player, fancy-coffee drinker, beach fanatic, lake and boat lover, and more. A woman who mattered. A woman who had purpose.

Most importantly, I was also a beloved daughter of the King. Although my worldly role and title had changed, my identity in Christ remained the same and was secure.

Paul shared this truth with the church in Ephesus and explained the new identity given to people when they are in Christ: "God had already decided that through Jesus Christ he would make us his children—this was his pleasure and purpose" (Eph. 1:5 GNT). Paul wanted believers to know that they would always be chosen, adopted, loved unconditionally, and accepted by God and that it pleased Him to call them His own.

If we as believers don't fully embrace our identity as children of God, we become vulnerable to letting circumstances, changes in titles and roles, life transitions, and other people's hurtful words or actions determine our identity and self-worth instead. What we do or don't achieve, what our title or role is or isn't, and what others think about us do not define who we are. Only God does. He is the source of our identity.

Sweet friend, **never measure your worth based on what an ex-spouse thinks of you**. Never measure your worth based on what you see in the mirror, your accomplishments, or your mistakes or failures. Instead, let God's Word be the only measuring stick you use, and remember, you can begin each new day with a clean slate.

God created women to be nurturing, and normally we take on that characteristic fully as wives, mothers, caretakers, or friends.

These are all wonderful things, but we often lose touch with who we really are and who we want to be. Many of us may come to realize we've lost our true selves because we spent so many years—at times decades—taking care of others' needs and never putting ourselves first. Or as I mentioned earlier, we carry around so much emotional baggage from our failed relationships that we've lost sight of the beautiful woman lying underneath the ruins.

 Let God's Word be the only measuring stick you use.

After divorce, we often have more time to ourselves than normal, so what better time to embrace the challenge of rediscovering both of our identities—who we are, and who we are in Christ? This time gives us breathing room to rediscover our true selves and do things we used to enjoy—things we didn't have time for before while prioritizing other demands of life. Most importantly, this time stirs our hearts to begin to accept that although our marriage died, we did not, and we still have a lot of life to live.

Some days will be easier than others, but you will always carry a part of the loss with you—because it happened and it's part of your story. Some level of your grief will always be in your heart, just as it would be if someone you loved had physically passed away. It will linger, and you will need strength and perseverance to keep going. Acceptance doesn't mean you're over it and you just go on without thinking about it. Acceptance does mean you are ready to embrace the life you have even if it's not the life you once imagined.

The Time Comes to Move Forward

The longer I continued in limbo with false hope, refusing to accept my marriage was over and continually hoping my husband would change and life would change, the more miserable I became. I felt depressed longer than I needed to simply because I couldn't accept that the end had come. My brain couldn't comprehend the death of my marriage and the life I had known for more than twenty-five years. I know a lot of women experience this same thing. I've even met women who stayed separated for years before getting divorced, even living in the same home with their husbands as nothing more than roommates, because they couldn't let themselves believe they would be okay without their spouses. They could have been leap years ahead in their journey had they come to a place of full acceptance sooner and made the hard but necessary choice to accept the marriage was over.

I am in no way encouraging divorce, and I pray every marriage can be saved. If both spouses have the willingness to work on themselves and the relationship, restoration can happen. But in many cases, restoration is not only impossible but also may not be in the best interest of the parties involved.

The divorce rates in our world today are astonishing and sad, and Christians are no exception. Christians are humans too and experience many of the same problems that non-Christians do in marriage. For Christians, marriage is a sacred covenant made before God in which two become one, but I also believe there are times when God is okay with that covenant being broken, in certain circumstances, and Scripture confirms this.

If you're anything like me, you may wonder, *Will God turn His back on me if I get divorced?* or *Doesn't God hate divorce and people who get divorced?* These were two of my most difficult fears to manage. As a Christian writer and speaker as well as a staff member at Proverbs 31 Ministries, I was worried about what people would think and whether I could still serve in ministry. *Am I worthy to serve God as a single, divorced woman?* I certainly didn't feel worthy. Instead, I felt ashamed and embarrassed. I felt like a failure, which was merely one of the dozens of negative descriptions I labeled myself with. And these feelings are all too common among women going through divorce.

Sadly, over the past few years, I've received countless emails from women around the world asking me the same questions, struggling to understand if their failed marriages meant they had a scarlet letter emblazoned on their chests in the eyes of God. I've also received emails from women suffering from all kinds of abuse, some who were living with husbands who were continually unfaithful and others who were just going through the motions in a loveless marriage year after year. All asking if Scripture says they had to stay in their marriage, no matter what, if they had to endure the abuse because of the covenant they made at the altar, and if God would still love them if they chose not to continue with their marriage.

The answer to all these questions is *absolutely not.*

God Does Not Hate You

In Malachi 2:16 we read that God hates divorce: "'I hate divorce!' says the LORD, the God of Israel." But often the next part of the verse is overlooked: "'To divorce your wife is to overwhelm her with cruelty,' says the LORD of Heaven's Armies. 'So guard your heart; do not be unfaithful to your wife.'" This verse actually applies to both husbands and wives because cruelty from either party breaks God's heart. You see, God simply hates what divorce stands for and knows it causes extensive problems, pain, and suffering for all involved. He doesn't want that for any of us.

Although God doesn't condone divorce, this verse doesn't imply in any way that God hates the people involved in a divorce regardless of the reason it happens. He is a forgiving and loving God who loves His children no matter what. He hates divorce because He knows it destroys people economically, emotionally, physically, psychologically, and sometimes even spiritually.

God loves you, whatever your marital situation, sins, or failures may be. Don't ever doubt that truth, and don't let anyone convince you otherwise. Put your faith in the biblical truth that God will never leave you even if your spouse did (see Heb. 13:5). He will also never leave you even if you left your spouse. We can survive by accepting what has happened and embracing life to the fullest no matter what it looks like.

 God loves you, whatever your marital situation, sins, or failures may be.

Allowing ourselves to finally accept the unacceptable or the unwanted is beyond difficult. It's hard to grieve the loss of someone who is alive and well. It's painful to release the dreams we once had and invite God to fill our lives with new dreams. Yet it's all necessary if our desire is to pick ourselves up no matter how hard we've been knocked down and take back control of our lives and our happiness.

God will open the door to the new life that awaits, but we have to choose to walk through that door. My prayer is that by the time you flip to the last page of this book, you will be ready to do exactly that.

Put One Foot in Front of the Other

You may always wonder about and secretly wish for what could have been. I know I do. No matter what stage you are in, even though you may not always be thinking about it, grief will still be there. It is for me. It may show up in waves some days or when a memory, movie, the thought of a lost dream, or certain situation triggers it, or you may go days without thinking about it at all.

You may think you're doing so much better but then suddenly find yourself grieving the missing plate at the dinner table, the empty seat beside you at a party, or the vacant side of the bed. You may long for the voice or laugh you never hear anymore. You may grieve the absence of someone to give you a hug and tell you it's going to be okay when you're going through something difficult. You will mourn not being a couple now that you're single. You will grieve not having a hand to hold as you walk on the beach at sunset with the waves lapping at your feet. You may experience a rush of sadness when loneliness creeps in like a thief of joy and it seems everyone has someone special except for you.

You may grieve the past. You may wish you had made different choices, which might have prevented this pain. If you're an empty-nester mom like me, you will likely grieve the days gone by when the kids were small and life was busy but full. If you're a mom of young kids, you may grieve the presence of a father in your children's lives as they grow and develop into mature adults.

If you're retired, you may feel completely bewildered and afraid of spending your retirement years as a single person.

Grief is a painful reality of the end of a marriage no matter what season we are in, but it paves the way for us to move forward as believers and accept what has happened. It empowers us to keep putting one foot in front of the other, believing that every step, no matter how small, is a step forward. We will always have God by our side, regardless of what stage we are struggling through or how long we've been there. And that should bring comfort.

> Embrace the life you have even if it's not the life you once imagined.

Second Corinthians 1:3–4 says, "All praise to God, the Father of our Lord Jesus Christ. God is our merciful Father and the source of all comfort. He comforts us in all our troubles so that we can comfort others. When they are troubled, we will be able to give them the same comfort God has given us." Paul was saying that not only is God fully capable of comforting us in our grief but that He is also a loving, kind, compassionate God. He is our source of comfort when we need it, and He will continue to hold us up as long as we need Him to. With Him by our side, we are never alone on the journey of mending our hearts and restoring our lives. With grounded faith and a commitment to ourselves, we can be unbroken once and for all. Just keep putting one foot in front of the other, and before long, you'll realize you really are making strides.

My prayer is that these words have planted a seed of hope. Knowing someone else understands, you will be able to take the first step in your journey of healing, overcoming, and thriving. We're in this thing together, my friend. It's going to get better from here. Stick with me.

Happiness Prompters

- Make a list of all the things that bring you joy in this season. Next time you're feeling down, pull out your list as a reminder of all the reasons you have to be happy. Each time you think of something new, add it to the list. This list will be your daily reminder of God's goodness during this stormy season of life.
- Write down the names of three people who make you happy; then give them a call.

Healing Steps

1. You can't write a new chapter of life until you stop rereading the last one. Consider whether you're holding on to any thoughts, feelings, or dreams that are keeping you from accepting the reality of your situation and moving on. In your journal, write down all the thoughts or feelings you're having a hard time releasing. Lay them at the foot of the cross in prayer, and ask God to help you embrace what is and let go of what can no longer be.

2. Think about how much happier you could feel if you decided to embrace your new normal and live with joy and hope, even if your circumstances remain the same. How would this change in you have a positive impact on your life and the lives of your children, friends, and other family members?

3. If you've been struggling with your identity, sit down and make a list of everything that makes you *you*. It's important to rediscover your identity and to realize this is a great time to become who you want to be. Spend time thinking about the new you and how you want to think, feel, and live. Then formulate some personal goals to help you get there.

Caring for You

What is one small thing you can start doing this week to take better care of yourself? What is something that would make you feel happy enough to not think about your circumstances, even for a brief time? Once you determine what you can do and want to do, make an appointment with yourself to do it. Put it on your calendar and make it a priority.

Chapter 3

Your Fears Are No Match for God

Overpowering negative emotions seemed to be running my life. After nearly a year of feeling exhausted, afraid, sad, and hopeless, I was ready to stop feeling exhausted, afraid, sad, and hopeless. I didn't want to live that way, and I knew that every day spent sad and afraid was another day wasted mourning instead of living.

I needed to retake control of my thoughts and my life. I was tired of letting my feelings boss me around, and I longed to break free from their stronghold over my mind and my life—and over my peace, joy, and happiness. Either I could control my mind, or it would continue to control me. I could live every day to the fullest—or not. The choice was mine.

One morning I felt more directionless and anxious than ever and decided to spend some time in deep prayer. I bowed my head and, like a broken record, began to remind God of all the challenges I was facing and how lost and hopeless I felt, as if He hadn't heard my hundreds of prayers that sounded the exact same. I expressed how tired I was of feeling tired. How emotionally exhausted I was and how fed up I was with feeling and living like a broken, discarded woman who had no hope for a bright future.

Tears fell as I called out from the pit for God to open my eyes and help me see His rays of hope. Then, suddenly, my heart and words began to shift. I found myself asking God for something different. Rather than listing my problems and asking Him to fix them as usual, I pleaded for insight about what to change within myself. I pleaded for Him to show me the true source of all my anxiety and any roadblocks to my healing and peace. I asked Him to make it clear to me what I needed to do and what I must let go of in order to heal, accept my situation, and be happy again. I shifted my prayer to what *I* needed to do instead of telling Him what I needed *Him* to do for me.

Countless thoughts flooded my mind. My heart began to pound as images of all the problems I was facing raced through the corridors of my brain. It felt as if I were being chased down a dark alley by the shadows of all my fears. So. Many. Shadows.

Our minds can sometimes be our worst enemy, especially when it comes to fear.

I had desperately needed Him to show me what was keeping me from His peace and being able to trust that things would be okay. I needed spiritual vision to see clearly, and it was in that divine moment when, as if scales fell from my eyes, I could see clearly for the first time. God helped me realize I had been struggling with many negative thought patterns, which were keeping me in a state of hopelessness. Fretting with deep angst over all the problems I had no power to solve. Worried to death about a million things, which made my heart and mind heavy every day. I came to the stark realization that one thing in particular had a life-robbing chokehold on my peace and my ability to move forward:

Fear.

Suffocating fears about the present day and the future would rob me of sleep at night and crush my spirit every morning before I even got out of bed. Fears about how my children were feeling and coping tore at my heart. Fears about how their heartbreak over the situation could scar them emotionally and affect their future relationships. Fears about being a good-enough mom and how I would handle being a single parent. Fears about finances and not being able to pay the bills. Fears about loneliness and being alone. Fears about what I was losing. Fears about things I never even thought about before all this happened.

Countless fears invaded my thoughts, rising higher and more toxic than massive garbage piles in a landfill. Fears that would always morph in my mind the more I thought about them, luring me into obsessing over all the horrific what-ifs. Nine times out of ten, my what-ifs were followed by panic-inducing thoughts of every worst-case scenario theory possible, which only served to pull me deeper into sadness, depression, and anxiety, even if those thoughts weren't rational.

Our minds can sometimes be our worst enemy, especially when it comes to fear.

The Sweetness of Surrender

Like a slap across the face, the hot sting of realizing the power my fears had been having on my life and my happiness was deep. It was

fear which had been powerfully keeping me stuck in the middle of
my grief and was standing in the way of accepting what had happened and trusting God for the future.

My fearful and negative thoughts had prevented me from believing that the end of the life I once knew did not mean my life had
ended. It didn't mean the future couldn't be great; it would just be
different than I had planned.

Tears began to flow yet again, but tears are necessary for healing.
According to an article in *Psychology Today*, they are like a release
valve for our stress, sadness, anxiety, and grief. Reflex tears (released
when our eyes are irritated) are 98 percent water, whereas "emotional
tears also contain stress hormones that get excreted from the body
through crying." Crying is not a sign of weakness but a sign that our
bodies need to excrete toxins that build up during times of immense
stress. Additionally, "studies ... suggest that crying stimulates the
production of endorphins, our body's natural pain killer and 'feel
good' hormones."[1] No wonder we feel so much better after having
a good cry!

My friend Debbie once told me that during a time when she
was struggling with her divorce situation and crying once again, "the
Lord whispered to me that we see clearer through tears. Perception
of reality somehow gets clearer when we deeply feel." I loved this
statement because it is so true.

So, as my tears dripped onto my lap, I intentionally, out loud
to God, committed to working on controlling my thoughts so they
didn't control my life anymore. I knew I needed to surrender all the
fears that had built up in my head for months to the only One who
was capable of carrying them.

I pulled out a tissue and wiped my eyes, then opened my laptop to where I kept my running digital journal of this nightmare I couldn't wake up from. As a writer, pouring words onto the screen was a healing balm to my soul, a place to let everything out without any regard to what anyone else might think. A safe place, where God and I could meet each day.

I began to type out my fears one by one as they came to mind, and what I witnessed was shocking. To my surprise, within a mere couple of minutes, I had written out thirty-three fears. Fears that slid easily off my fingers onto the keyboard. I probably could have kept going, but I paused and stared in awe at the list on my screen.

Thirty. Three. Paralyzing. Fears. Have mercy.

I didn't realize until that moment how my fears had multiplied and mutated into an invisible monster that was choking the life out of me. I had no idea how much they were damaging my attitude, thoughts, emotions, and perspectives, and affecting how I was living my everyday life.

Immediately I surrendered those fears and all the accompanying emotions in prayer. I spoke all thirty-three aloud individually and laid them at the feet of Jesus, one by one. I longed to break free from fear, anxiety, and hopelessness and grab on to His hope instead. I wanted to see that light at the end of the tunnel, even if it was just a tiny flicker. I committed right then and there, to God and to myself, to take a firm stand against letting all those fears slip back into my subconscious and snuff out my peace.

Slowly yet assuredly, as the days and weeks passed, I began to deliberately capture fearful thoughts before they crushed my spirit or threatened my peace. As I tried to think more positively every time a situation would upset me and intentionally choose to trust God with a certain fear that made my heart race, my attitude began to change. My chest began to feel less tight. My stomach less in knots. My breath flowed more easily. My mind was at ease and my heart felt lighter because I was allowing God to replace my mental chaos with His calm.

Daily I invited God to help me transform my thoughts. I consistently asked for His peace even when fear was staring me in the face, and He never failed to answer that prayer.

The difference that prayer of surrender made in my outlook and in my life was astonishing. I now understand how we can have a peace that surpasses understanding in the midst of tragedy (see Phil. 4:7).

Peace Does Come

The Bible has a lot to say about fear, but one of my favorite passages is found in the book of Isaiah.

> Fear not, for I am with you;
>   be not dismayed, for I am your God;
> I will strengthen you, I will help you,
>   I will uphold you with my righteous right hand.
>   (Isa. 41:10 ESV)

These words were primarily directed to the Jews who would face a difficult captivity in Babylon. God was reminding them that they were His and, therefore, they had nothing to fear. You and I are also His. Therefore, we have nothing to fear either.

Yet even understanding this scriptural truth, I know it's still hard not to live afraid of the what-ifs and unknowns. When the life we thought was all secure and planned out becomes nothing more than a big tangle of heartache, problems, fears, and crushed dreams, how do we avoid being fearful of the future?

God's promise to be with His beloveds, to strengthen those who need strength, and to uphold them with His righteous hand is as valid for us today as it was for the Jews back then. We won't always be protected from situations that elicit fear; in fact, we never will be. Difficulties and unknowns are a normal part of life. Yet we can always surrender our fears to God and trust that He will never leave our side. We can remember that He is more than capable of handling whatever problems fill our hearts and minds with fear and giving us the strength to persevere. In fact, we are reminded not only that He is capable but also that when we feel the weakest, He is the strongest. "My grace is all you need. My power works best in weakness" (2 Cor. 12:9).

Although most of my fear-induced emotions that fretful morning were valid, I had allowed them to take over my mind and, in turn, take over my life and my happiness, as well as rob me of much-needed sleep and rest.

Maybe today you are struggling with fear too. Maybe a lot of fears—thirty-three, fifty-three, or even one hundred and three. Maybe those fears are grounded in your divorce or another challenge in your life. Maybe you've received a concerning health diagnosis and you're scared of the outcome, a fear that is compounded by having no partner by your side. Maybe you're worried you'll be alone forever. Maybe your job is unstable or you don't have a job because you spent years raising your children and being a stay-at-home mom and wife. Maybe you have no idea how to pay all the bills and your ex is not providing as he should be, legally or ethically. Maybe the house is in foreclosure and you're scrambling to figure out where to live or what to do. Maybe your ex is violating court orders for alimony or child support but you don't have the money, much less the emotional energy, to fight the legal battle yet again.

Maybe the bank account is low, the refrigerator is empty, the kids need stuff for school or tuition for college, and you have no idea where money is going to come from. Maybe your children, big or small, are acting out, suffering emotionally, or struggling with what to believe and how to manage their feelings. Maybe you're facing the reality of figuring out co-parenting duties and schedules and the thought of being away from your kids during the holidays—or at all—is simply more than your heart can handle. Maybe your divorce happened at the age of retirement and you're wondering what you're going to do for the rest of your life without the person you planned on spending your golden years with. Maybe you have an empty nest for the first time and it's way too quiet.

> It's okay and normal to have fears, but it's not okay to let them have you.

These are just a tiny sampling of circumstances that produce valid fears and paralyzing emotions. Over time they become thick black clouds that seem to hover over our every waking moment and prevent us from seeing any sunshine at all.

Yet regardless of the scary unknowns and problems that seem large, looming, or hopeless right now, you can be free from fearing the worst. It's okay and normal to have fears, but it's not okay to let them have you. At some point we have to stop fearing all that could go wrong and start getting excited about all the good things God will do because He always has a plan and a purpose for our lives and our pain.

As believers, we all have the power of the Holy Spirit within us to break down the stronghold of fear and grab hold of the peace God offers. We can all surrender our fears to God if we choose to put our trust in Him instead of tossing and turning every night under the weight of worry. We have to realize our fears are there, recognize their power over our lives, and choose to hand them over to God.

You will experience fear when going through divorce, but **how wonderful could life be if you chose not to let those fears overshadow your faith and fully trusted God would take care of you?** How much happier would you feel if you no longer had to shoulder the burden of worry, always waiting for the other shoe to drop? This type of fearless living is possible when we surrender our fears to God and learn to believe He truly does have everything in His hands.

God is near to you, even if you can't feel Him. If He feels far away, bow your head right now and sit in His presence. He is at work in your life. He does have a good plan for you. He wants to alleviate your fears and fill you with that peace that surpasses understanding. The type of peace that will astound other people as they bear witness to your lack of fear, your unshakable joy, and your faithful trust in God as you walk the hardest road you've ever had to walk. God is your biggest supporter of starting anew, and He wants your heart to be free.

God Is Holding Your Future in His Hands

Based on my own experience and research, as well as conversations with many women, it seems there are many common fears that paralyze women when they face the end of a marriage. One of the top-named fears is fear of the future.

Recently I was reading back through my digital journal entries written shortly after my husband left, and I decided to do a search for the word *future*. When the results came up, I discovered I had written about fearing the future forty-seven times in just a few months. Gracious. I must confess, though—I have obsessed over what lies ahead hundreds if not thousands of times since then. Maybe you have too.

It's okay, because after all, who wouldn't fear the future when everything they knew and everything they thought would be is ripped out from under them? When a marriage ends, so many hopes and dreams are lost. The future looks bleak. Unknown. Terrifying.

I won't share all the journal entries with you, but I will share the end of the entry from that day when my thirty-three fears flowed onto the page. After typing them all out and recognizing the power they held over my peace, I typed out this prayer:

Wow. I have a lot of fears. Lord, I lay them down to You today. Please take them off my heart. Please. Replace them with peace, joy, and hope and an optimistic vision for the future. Change my heart to be positive, even though my life is negative right now. Help me notice when You are working in me and around me. Help my kids; give them peace. Help me be the mom they need me to be. Help me to take my eyes off my hurt and feelings and experience theirs. Help me know what to do. Help me be their friend, confidant, supporter, and encourager—not the one who makes things hard for them with my outpouring of anger, hurt, fears, and emotions. Lift all these fears off my heart, because they are fueling worry, overwhelming worry that consumes my every thought every day. Lord, I release each one to You today. I release ... [and then I listed them]. Amen.

That evening I went to bed and slept better than I had in months. When I awoke the next day, I felt a peace I hadn't felt in a long time. I didn't dread getting out of bed and facing the day. I didn't feel heavy or tired. Hopelessness and worry didn't take my breath away before my bare feet hit the floor. Peace allowed hope to grow in my weary soul.

When I awoke the next day, as I did every morning, I reached over to my nightstand and opened my *Jesus Calling* devotion. I flipped to the correct date, and my heart leaped. It was as if God were speaking right to my heart with words of assurance I needed right that minute.

> I am your Refuge and Strength, an ever-present Help in trouble. Therefore, you don't need to be afraid of anything—not even cataclysmic circumstances.... If you ... forget that I am your Refuge in all circumstances, you will become increasingly fearful. Every day I manifest My grace in countless places and situations.... I shower not only blessings but also outright miracles on your planet.
>
> As you grow closer to Me, I open your eyes to see more and more of My Presence all around you. Things that most people hardly notice, like shifting shades of sunlight, fill you with heart-bursting Joy. You have eyes that see and ears that hear, so

proclaim My abiding Presence in the world. Psalm
46:1–3; Psalm 89:15–16[2]

I believe God wanted me to know He saw me. He saw me typing
out my fears. He saw me struggling to turn them over but heard
my pleas for intervention. He saw my tears and caught them, just
as we're told in Psalm 56:8: "You keep track of all my sorrows. You
have collected all my tears in your bottle." I believe He was whispering, *"Tracie, trust that I am with you, protecting you, and I'm going
before you in every circumstance, just as I promise in My Word."* I was
reminded of Deuteronomy 31:8: "Do not be afraid or discouraged,
for the LORD will personally go ahead of you. He will be with you;
he will neither fail you nor abandon you."

This sweet encounter with God helped me begin to understand
why I didn't need to continue living in fear of the future, feeling
powerless and hopeless. I just needed to have faith that He was one
step ahead of me, every day in everything, and that I could find
courage through His encouragement.

Whatever your situation and however long your list of fears is, will
you allow yourself to believe God has your future in His hands? That
He has a plan for you? That He hasn't abandoned you and never will?
Girl, He's got this. Will you believe it? Somehow He always takes care
of His daughters, and He already has your future all planned out.

God Will Provide for Your Needs

Financial instability is the second most common fear after divorce,
especially if the spouse has essentially abandoned all obligations.
Nobody wants to be broken and broke.

For the first several months after we separated, things went okay. Bills were still getting paid, but I worried daily about what might happen if he stopped providing. In less than six months, my worst fears came true. Financial support stopped coming without any notice or explanation. After several months of no income, pure panic began to overtake my soul. I hadn't worked full time in twelve years, as I had stayed home to raise my children and focus on speaking and writing, so I soon had to cash out my 401(k) and pension plans from prior jobs and depend on savings to provide for our needs. But that money quickly dwindled. This level of abandonment compounded my devastation, and the pain in my heart grew deeper and heavier than I even thought possible.

I was counting the days until the power would be cut off and stressing over where we would live if the house was foreclosed on. Constantly juggling money, just trying to stay afloat and keep my children's lives as normal as possible. My financial fears became suffocating.

I imagine you may have experienced these types of fears too. In fact, maybe you are experiencing them right now, and if so, I want to reassure you with one of the most precious promises we glean from Scripture:

God always provides. Always. Without fail. Pause right now, close your eyes, and repeat those words. *God always provides. Always. Without fail.* "This same God who takes care of me will supply all your needs from his glorious riches, which have been given to us in Christ Jesus" (Phil. 4:19). When we put our faith in Christ, God commits to love, protect, and provide.

In my case, unexpected checks arrived out of nowhere, always just in the nick of time, such as refunds from accounts I didn't know had been overpaid or a royalty check from the sales of one of my books. Friends and family members stepped forward to help financially, at times even without being asked or knowing the severity of my situation. Miracles occurred with the mortgage company to help me get my home out of the foreclosure process over time. After months of searching for employment, all the while growing weary and losing self-confidence and hope, I received a perfect job offer—on my birthday. I also received the opportunity to do some writing and training projects, which brought in additional income.

> Whatever your situation and however long your list of fears is, will you allow yourself to believe God has your future in His hands?

God recently amazed me, yet again, with His provision and protection. I had been fighting a long, hard, seemingly hopeless legal battle with regards to my home. The circumstances were so far beyond my ability to fix them, I had succumbed to believing they could never be resolved. Four years had passed, and I had given up all hope. But then, a prayer that seemed unanswerable, even by an almighty God, was answered in a way I could never have imagined or orchestrated on my own. He pieced together the perfect people, connections, and timing, and it was nothing short of a miracle. I stood shocked and in awe and immediately broke out in tears of joy. But I also felt regretful for doubting God's faithfulness. For not fully believing He knew my needs and would take care of them, in His timing and in His perfect way. I gave Him all the credit and all the praise.

Sometimes we forget God can be trusted with the biggest of problems—even the ones that seem insurmountable—especially when we feel our prayers are going unheard while our problems keep pressing in on us from every side. Scripture tells us nothing is impossible for God (see Luke 1:37 ESV), but in the weakness of our humanity and the pools of hopelessness we get caught up in, we forget that all too often.

I couldn't begin to list all the examples of God's unexplainable provision in my life. There are still prayers on my heart, issues to resolve, and problems to overcome, but over the past few years, I've watched God weave His goodness and faithfulness into the fabric of my messed-up life, and it has raised my faith in His provision to an all-time high.

The Joy in Seeing God's Provision

Several of my friends have been through difficult divorces as well, so I asked them if they would be willing to share how God provided for them in special ways. Their answers blew me away.

Christine had just begun to attend a new church and hadn't shared her financial struggles with anyone. On her way to church one Sunday, she felt inner turmoil about tithing. After all, she had $80 to her name, which needed to last another two weeks for necessities. Pushing aside her excuses and hesitations, she put it in the offering plate, admitting to having little faith God would actually provide. After church the pastor pulled her aside and said God had placed her name on the hearts of the elders earlier that week, and he handed her an envelope—with a beautiful card and exactly $80 inside.

Malinda had $6 to her name on the day her office threw a small party to celebrate her relocation to a new department within her company. Without anyone knowing her needs, her coworkers gave her a sweet card of congratulations with $100 tucked inside.

Michelle struggled to pay the bills after her husband's abandonment. Out of the blue, she heard from their business accountant that a credit had been missed for three years, resulting in a refund of several thousand dollars. God knew what she needed and when she would need it, and He had put a plan in place years earlier to meet her needs at the very moment she needed it most.

Holly secretly fretted daily about how to pay the bills because she was too embarrassed to let anyone know her situation and didn't want to ask for help. She opened her front door one morning to find an anonymous card on her doorstep with $300 in it and three beautiful words: *You are loved.*

Becky had been cleaning the house of an elderly couple for years. One day God impressed upon the husband of that couple to pay off her car loan because he knew she was struggling financially as a single mom, leaving her in awe of God's faithfulness.

Diana was living without basic necessities due to being injured at work and receiving only a small workers' comp check each month. One day a total stranger put a tube of toothpaste in her mailbox. She had never been so thankful for toothpaste. Another time a church member surprised her family with a box of food and a $150 gift card to the grocery store.

Someone donated a car to Jennifer—yes, a car! Later, when the brakes went out, the Lord directed someone to leave an anonymous $500 check for her at the mechanic's shop. Right when she had no money to buy groceries for her family. And Shelly received a large unexpected check from her mortgage company for an overpayment on an escrow account.

If your financial situation seems hopeless and scary right now, I pray hearing these true stories of God's provision will infuse hope and comfort into your heart. However, you might be thinking, *Why did God answer their prayers and not mine? Why haven't I seen a financial miracle from God?* Or *Why am I still struggling? Is my faith not strong enough?*

It's hard to be happy for people who receive miraculous blessings when we are praying for miracles in our own lives and don't see them happening. I want to encourage you to pray about pushing those thoughts aside while you're waiting on God to answer, remembering He hears your prayers and is not turning a deaf ear. In fact, He may answer your prayers in a way and at a time that you didn't expect, but it will be miraculous nonetheless.

God Always Knows Best

God's provision is not always financial. My friend Denise prayed so long for reunification with her husband, but her prayer was never answered. Her divorce went through, and she found herself a single mom. She may have felt as if God didn't hear her prayers, and I completely understand that. I did not see my prayers for reconciliation answered in my marriage either. But Denise shared that now God has given her greater peace and happiness than she ever experienced while she was married. He knew what was best for her and her future.

She also shared how, when she was looking for a new home, a contract on the house she so desperately wanted fell through. She had prayed relentlessly for God to bless her with this home, but that prayer went unanswered, and disappointment ran deep. But then she found a better house, which was the perfect size for her and her entire family, with precious neighbors and fellow prayer warriors who are always there for her. Neighbors she would have never met had she closed on the other house. God showed off even more by placing her new home within walking distance of her new church. Her words to me were "I've quit doubting God always provides! Finally!"

Even when we think God is doing one thing, He could be doing something else entirely. This happened to Debbie after her divorce. Debbie was praying for reconciliation, believing God was orchestrating that outcome, as she began to fall back in love with her ex-husband and believe he still loved her. Until another woman came into the picture and he walked away—again. Clearly that looked like a crushing unanswered prayer, and Debbie was devastated. But her life now reflects something far from devastation.

Today she has joy, contentment, and peace with God, her life, and herself that she would never have had if she had stayed in that relationship. She said she is better off now and is thankful that God's plan, although much different from what she thought she wanted, was so much better than hers.

Perhaps not every person we lose is a loss. Sometimes God may allow people to leave our lives because He knows He has something even better in store for us.

He hears your prayers and is not turning a deaf ear.

Cyndi told me she often felt God wasn't hearing or answering her prayers, not just about her marital situation but about life in general. But He proved faithful time and time again. She prayed for a job she didn't get, only to get a much better job a few months later. She couldn't sell her home when she wanted to and didn't get the new home she wanted, only to end up a few years later in her dream home. She prayed for God to protect her womb as she struggled with having a baby, but she still had several miscarriages. Why would God not answer her prayers for a baby? Maybe He had a better plan. She adopted a precious little boy in need of a family, who is the joy of her life and now twenty-one years old. None of these things were her plans or her prayers, but God's plans and answers were so much better.

We are only human, so doubting God's provision in every way is only natural. Worry fuels fear, and fear is built into our makeup as a survival instinct. It's always going to be present, but we can keep it at bay by continually remembering His faithfulness and choosing to trust He is working behind the scenes on our behalf.

If you find yourself doubting God's love and plans for you, don't beat yourself up. Fear is life robbing and doubt inducing, but remembering that God has provided for His children in incredible ways—from biblical times to the present day—helps us cling to hope. He will provide for you too, precious friend—financially, spiritually, emotionally, and physically.

We are all called to believe without seeing; however, it can be so hard to do. Yet when we see Him at work so mightily and supernaturally, faith can soar and trust will grow. Waiting is hard, but God is always dependable, and His timing is always perfect.

Provision. Strength. Peace. Hope. Companionship. Joy. Courage. He is able to provide all these things and more. Trust that He is at work even if you don't see anything happening right now.

Taking Back the Power

Women struggle with countless other fears in addition to those about finances and the future. For example, the fear of having friends or family turn their backs on us in our time of greatest pain and need. I regret to say I have experienced this, and it hurts. All contact with my in-laws ceased the day after my husband left, and I had loved them for nearly three decades. Friends who had been in my life since college cut themselves off from me and even my children, who had grown up knowing and loving them. And other friends gradually backed away, saying they couldn't hang out with a single woman since they were married. People often don't realize the pain their words and actions can cause an already-wounded soul.

None of this seemed fair, especially since I was not the one who had caused our marriage breakup, nor did I choose to be single. But I realized God had spent years bringing wonderful friends into my life—friends who would stand by me through thick and thin, no matter how hard it got. Friends and loved ones who wouldn't leave me just because my marital status changed. Although it was painful to have that handful of people turn their backs on me, it was such sweet comfort to see how God had been preparing me for this season for many years.

God knew what would happen—who would stay in my life and who would leave—and He had already filled in the gaps for when I would need devoted, loving friends the most. He also blessed me with a wonderful family and three amazing grown children. After a while, I chose to focus on and be thankful for the blessing of who *was* in my life instead of fretting over the few who weren't.

Other common fears include the fear of being a single mom, which is hard no matter how old your children are. The fear of what other people think about you and gossip that might be going around. The fear of people not understanding what really happened and making their own assumptions. Fears about how divorce will affect your children's hearts and their view of marriage, how they allow others to treat them, and their future relationships. The fear of an ex-husband bringing another woman into your children's lives or creating a new family with them, just without you. The fear of change. The fear of not knowing who you are anymore. The fear of being alone forever. The fear of never being happy again or finding love.

I could write page after page on dealing with specific fears and the emotions and pain associated with each one. But I don't want to do that. Instead, I want to focus on how to move past fear and embrace happiness. It's necessary to acknowledge the pain and fears that a failed marriage brings, but it's not necessary to get stuck in that muck.

It's time to start focusing on the positives. From this point on in these pages, we are going to start climbing the mountain. Ascending to a place where we can let go of the fear and leave the pain behind, feel closer to God, see life from a new perspective, embrace loving ourselves again, start building a new life, and begin to accept the new reality we are living in with hearts of joy and minds full of peace and hopeful expectations.

It is possible to feel happy and live a happy life post-divorce, and I hope the upcoming chapters will help you realize it's possible for you.

In the words of Max Lucado, "Feed your fears and your faith will starve. Feed your faith and your fears will."[3] Friend, let's start doing that today. There is no better time than the present to let go of your fears, focus on feeding your faith, and start taking back your happiness.

Happiness Prompters

- Make a list of all the people in your life right now who bring you joy, comfort, conversation, friendship, love, understanding, and companionship. Those people who have stood beside you through thick and thin and love you no matter what. Then, beside each name, write what they mean to you, how they positively affect your life, or the blessings you receive from your relationship with them. Thank God in prayer for each of these precious people He placed into your presence for such a time as this, and maybe even consider letting them know how important they are to you, especially if you haven't told them lately.

- Consider issues you worried about in the past that are not important now or fears you struggled with that never came to fruition. Were they worth worrying about? Did worrying change anything? If not, how might acknowledging this fact change your perception about what you're worrying about right now?

Healing Steps

1. In your quiet time, ask God to bring to your mind all the fears weighing on your heart. Keep writing them down one by one as you think of them, coming back to your list over the next couple of days, if needed. Spend some time in prayer surrendering them to Him. Ask Him to fill you with a peace that surpasses understanding.

2. Start a "Provisions List" on a piece of paper, and place it somewhere you see frequently—in your journal, on your bathroom mirror, or on your refrigerator. Each time you witness God providing for you—spiritually, emotionally, physically, or financially—record it so you'll never forget.

3. Close your eyes, and envision who and where you'd like to be this time next year. Think about how you would like to be feeling, living, working, and achieving. Dare to dream and imagine yourself enjoying these dreams coming true. Allow the space between

where you are today and where you want to be to inspire you to
keep pushing forward.

Caring for You

How is stress potentially affecting your mental state as well as
your health? Do some online research about the toll stress takes
on our bodies, and let the facts be your motivation to continually surrender your fears to God rather than letting them keep
you awake at night and damage your health. You can also check
out my book *Stressed-Less Living: Finding God's Peace in Your
Chaotic World* for more tips and encouragement about managing stress.

Chapter 4

Overcoming Loneliness

After divorce, loneliness will most assuredly strike.

When you go from having a spouse at home every night for years to sitting at home every night alone with your thoughts, the poison of loneliness can make you feel as if you'll never survive. But regardless of whether divorce is the root cause, loneliness has become an epidemic in our society and it can affect us physically, mentally, and emotionally.

Steve Cole, professor of medicine, psychiatry, and biobehavioral sciences at UCLA, did a study in which he looked at white blood cell samples from men and women who identified as being lonely. He was startled to discover that in each sample "the blood cells appeared to be in a state of high alert, responding the way they would to a bacterial infection." Cole's research showed that "it was as though the subjects were under mortal assault by a disease—the disease of loneliness."[1] But in Christ, no matter what we're struggling with, we can overcome.

A senior research scientist at the University of Chicago stated that loneliness "is a universal human experience, and being the social animals that we are, there must be implications when those social connections are not satisfied." She also noted that when our human need for connection is not satisfied, "the consequences are very real in terms of mental and physical health."[2] In fact, researchers at the AARP Public Policy Institute, Stanford, and Harvard found that social isolation increases the cost of Medicare by $6.7 billion a year, primarily because of longer hospital stays that could be caused by "a lack of community support."[3]

In 2018, a nationwide survey of twenty thousand adults showed that "54% of respondents said they feel like no one actually knows them well" and "56% of people said the people they surround themselves [with] 'are not necessarily with them.'" They also discovered "approximately 40% said they 'lack companionship,' their 'relationships aren't meaningful,' and that they feel 'isolated from others.'"[4]

Although this survey doesn't specify the percentage of the participants who were separated or divorced, I can only imagine they make up a good portion of those battling this epidemic based on the divorce rates in today's society.

Researchers continue to discover more information about the alarming number of people who feel lonely and how loneliness attacks our bodies and shortens lives. An AARP article noted, "Loneliness is a killer—an array of studies have found that it leaves us more likely to die from heart disease and is a contributing factor in other fatal conditions. It makes us more vulnerable to Alzheimer's disease, high blood pressure, suicide, even the common cold."[5] All proof you can actually die from a broken heart.

Loneliness takes a silent toll on people, and it is not something to be ignored. It is an issue every separated or divorced person struggles with at one time or another, and there is no rhyme or reason about how and when it will affect us. None of these statistics are fun, positive information, to say the least. But the good news is that it is possible to be alone without being overcome by loneliness. It takes time, but as our hearts and minds heal, we can win our battle with loneliness.

> *Both physical and mental isolation cause us to feel completely alone and prevent anyone from being able to support or encourage us in our internal battle to survive.*

The struggle of loneliness in the early days of my separation is a vivid memory, as is a life-changing lesson I learned about myself along the way.

During the first six months after my husband moved out, I faced the toxicity of loneliness day in and day out. All my children had busy lives, I worked from home, and at night I typically stayed home and watched TV.

Both of my daughters were in college, and spring break rolled around. They had planned a short cruise with their friends and encouraged me to fly down to Florida to spend a day in the sun with them before they boarded the ship. I needed a break from life, if only for a couple of days, so I jumped at the opportunity.

The first day was filled with laughter and smiles. The Florida sunshine warmed me from the inside out, improving my mood and temporarily thawing the cold emptiness in my heart. The change of scenery and focus was exactly what I needed. But the following morning when it was time for my girls to leave for the ship with their friends, I sensed a heaviness building inside me. I kept it to myself because I so wanted them to enjoy a mini escape from the pain we had all been enduring. I also wanted to avoid making them feel sad about leaving me standing on the sidewalk waving good-bye. So I put on a fake smile and gave them each a big send-off hug (plus a few warnings about making good choices, of course!).

After the shuttle bus drove away, I turned to walk back into the hotel, and an overwhelming feeling of sadness and loneliness immediately permeated my soul.

At the onset, I thought I was just feeling envious that they were going on a Caribbean cruise and I was stuck going home to the broken mess called my life. But I soon realized it wasn't envy but instead a crushing awareness of being completely alone. On vacation. In another state. There I was, all by myself, six hundred miles from home and no way to get back until the next day when my flight was scheduled to depart.

I headed to the beach in an attempt to make the best of my time, but as I lay on the lounge chair, mesmerized with people-watching, I couldn't hold back the tears. Nobody else seemed to be alone on this beautiful, sunny spring day. Only me. I saw couples clearly in love, college students having fun, families building sandcastles together, and husbands and wives huddled on their towels, reading books, listening to music, and engaging in conversation. All the things I used to be and do. But now, it was just me and my chair.

The reality hit me like a punch in the gut—being alone was my permanent new normal.

I had already experienced intense loneliness due to my husband traveling five days a week for years, but I was now enduring a new kind of loneliness every day. One that I knew had no end in sight. I had already learned it was possible to feel as lonely when in a room full of people or in the den with my spouse as I did when physically alone. But this … felt different and excruciating. As if I had been dropped off on another planet and left there to survive. All alone.

Eventually I gathered my things and went back to the hotel, showered, and dressed for dinner, all the while grappling with the idea of just ordering room service and hiding under the bedcovers instead. I mean, seriously, who goes out to dinner by herself—on vacation no less? I felt sort of pathetic but decided to push past my emotions and muster the courage to go out to dinner alone.

I walked down the street and noticed an outdoor marina restaurant, with boats bobbing in the calm water and lights twinkling in the palm trees. Laughter, conversation, and music filled the salty air—all sounds I normally would adore but now only served to amplify my sense of aloneness. Rather than getting a table for one, I slid into an empty seat at the bar, where I ordered a glass of wine for me, myself, and I.

Shortly after, several people began talking with me, and conversations were pleasant. I made some new friends and began to feel less alone. The server was friendly and the food was delicious. My mood lifted, and I became acutely aware that I was actually enjoying myself and other people were enjoying my company. I felt a sense of pride for getting out, putting myself out there, and meeting new people. I gained a sense of empowerment that felt foreign in my insecure mind—and a newfound belief that maybe being alone wasn't the worst thing in the world after all. Something deep inside me shifted that night as God whispered to my heart, *"You're going to make it."*

The Faces of Loneliness

For me and many other women, loneliness usually peaks when we focus on an empty nest, an empty house, an empty spot at the dinner table, and/or an empty bed. It can spike for a single person at holidays, weddings, couples' events, concerts, parties, or even movies. But no matter how hard we try to avoid feeling lonely, every separated or divorced person experiences loneliness in some way, even if you wanted the marriage to end. Loneliness will look and feel different for everyone.

In the early days of her separation and divorce, my friend Lisa mentioned she often felt the loneliest on nights and weekends when she wanted someone to talk to or hang out with who understood her well. Not having someone to do the little things in life with—sharing household responsibilities, cooking dinner, watching television, holding hands—made those little things seem like big things, exacerbating her feelings of loneliness.

Chanda feels the most alone when her young children spend time with her ex-husband. Being without her children makes her feel she has nothing to do and no one to take care of, leaving her unsure of how to fill her time. As a single mom, Laura struggles when she feels exhausted and overwhelmed with her young kids and often finds herself feeling lonely and wishing she still had someone to help with things like baths, bedtime, sicknesses, tantrums, and so on. Malinda said weekends are hardest for her, because even though she has a desire to get out of the house and be with others, her financial situation often prevents her from doing so.

Rising Above

Regardless of how we experience loneliness, there are many ways to rise above it. Just as we all experience it differently, we all have different coping mechanisms. My first inclination is to spend time with my adult children, who have become my best friends. I've also been blessed with many girlfriends who have played a major role in my battle with loneliness over the years.

I love spending time with these precious women. We play tennis and rounds of golf, go to concerts, dine out, go on girls' trips, and attend tailgates and football games together. Sometimes we simply hang out in the backyard, listening to music and playing cornhole for hours on end. I've also taken up new hobbies and continue to pour myself into writing and ministry. I fill my time and keep busy as much as possible, and there actually are days when I look forward to snuggling into the couch with a good Netflix movie and a glass of wine. But there are also days when I still deeply feel the absence of a spouse, and loneliness feels like a tourniquet on my heart. On those days, I've learned to intentionally try to focus on doing something that will help me feel better rather than allowing myself to sink into my feelings.

Chanda confessed that when she's feeling lonely, she'll sometimes go to her office or walk around stores and window-shop to avoid being home alone and tempted to feel lonely.

My friend Debbie is a task-oriented person, so when she starts feeling the weight of loneliness, she sets a goal, even if it's just reading fifty pages of a book. Marilyn goes into crazy-lady cleaning mode to pass the time, and admittedly I have done that myself, which comes with the benefit of a spotless house!

Karen mentioned she combats her feelings of loneliness by reminding herself loneliness is not from God but from the enemy, who would like nothing more than to isolate her from God and others. She intentionally works on maintaining the mind-set she wants and needs in order to embrace her new normal, start new traditions, and even set goals to get involved in new ministries.

> Whether we are married, divorced, or single, God is the One who is always by our side.

Some people start new adventures. Karen and Tammy both registered for classes at a local college to pursue new careers and also started volunteering at local organizations. And when Becky starts feeling alone, she shifts her focus to gratitude and forces herself to think about all the things she has to be thankful for.

Natalie admitted her coping mechanism was often isolation. I too went through a phase of isolating myself when being in social settings seemed too hard and the awareness of not having a partner by my side would tug at my heart. Natalie also mentioned an important lesson she had learned. To avoid the temptation to stay in her house all alone, ultimately ending up feeling even lonelier, she made herself say yes to invitations from her friends even if nothing in her wanted to get out and go.

I loved how Natalie shared that after she would begrudgingly say yes and go out with her friends, ignoring that inner voice urging her to stay secluded in her home, she would be reminded time and time again that the enemy of our souls would have loved for her to stay isolated and depressed. She said, "When talking to friends about how I'm feeling—again—feels like the last thing I want to do and the last thing they want to hear, I found that is usually when I need to talk the most. I have to remind myself Satan would love for me to stay quiet and convince me that I'm in this all on my own."

Two Types of Being Alone

The word *isolation* means "the state of one who is alone."[6] However, isolation does not always mean locking yourself up in your house or office and staying away from people completely. Isolation can be one's physical situation, or it can be a mental situation. It can be locking up your willingness to share your feelings with others and be real, even when you're around others. It can also be putting on the "everything is fine" mask and acting as if you're handling your situation like a champ.

Both physical and mental isolation cause us to feel completely alone and prevent anyone from being able to support or encourage us in our internal battle to survive.

Unfortunately, I did both.

The first few months post-separation, I didn't want to be around people at all. I was emotionally unstable, to say the least, and didn't have the physical or emotional energy to hang out with friends, pretend I was fine, answer people's curious questions, or accept anyone's awkward condolences. But I felt incredibly lonely.

Not only did I stop social activities, but I also stopped going to church, simply because I couldn't bring myself to sit all alone in the same Sunday school class or the same pew where I had spent twenty years sitting with my husband and children. I couldn't bear to gaze across the sanctuary and see all the happy couples and families sitting together—God-fearing, devoted husbands and unbroken families— the scenarios my heart so desperately desired. I also wanted to avoid the high risk of anyone offering to pray for me or tell me they were sorry for what we were going through. That would have resulted in a meltdown with a full inability to regain any composure, likely humiliating myself and my children. Not that I don't believe people genuinely care about others who are suffering. That's usually why they ask how they're doing. But nobody wants to have too much messiness dumped on them, which would likely be more than they bargained for, prompting them to squirm for a way to retreat from the conversation.

I've always been a more quiet, private person, so opening up to people about my feelings and circumstances has never come easy. In the face of tragedy, weighed down by shame and embarrassment, I felt it was safer to be a recluse physically *and* emotionally, even with immediate family members. I rarely talked with anyone about how I felt, much less opened up about all the problems crashing in on me like a tsunami. Even if I was slowly dying inside and desperately craved words of advice, hope, and compassion to ease my aching soul, I continually held myself hostage behind the walls of isolation, which somehow seemed safer.

Trust that He has your future in His hands and that He hears the silent cries of your heart.

Both types of isolation—hiding away from people and wearing an "everything is fine" mask when I was around others—caused me much more harm than good.

After a while, I forced myself to get back out there and do life with others, spend time with friends and family, and visit new churches, but I still kept that champion mask on and hid my thoughts and emotions behind a wall nobody could penetrate. I didn't want to share my feelings or provide any updates on legal or money issues, even if someone was asking only because of how much he or she loved me and worried about me. As a result, people would continually tell me how strong I was, but inside, I was secretly a weak, broken mess.

Neither of these isolation tactics helped me move forward, and in hindsight, I could have used deeper support from friends, family, other believers, and especially from other women who were walking or had walked in my shoes. Yet it was my own fault for isolating myself. Today, those days when I don't feel like being around people are usually the days I need companionship and social interaction the most, so I try to push past the enemy's temptations to believe that I would be better off alone and just go.

God created us to crave companionship, and when our primary companion exits our lives, loneliness will strike. But there is good news.

You're Never Really Alone

After enjoying a delicious dinner and spirit-lifting conversation at the marina restaurant that night in Florida, I went back to the hotel and snuggled into bed. Slowly but surely, the feeling of deep-seated loneliness returned. But instead of crying and giving in to those thoughts, I immediately began to replay my eye-opening evening in my mind and shift my thoughts to prayer. Unexpectedly, like a warm blanket laid gently across my soul, I began to sense I wasn't alone after all.

Psalm 139 immediately floated into my thoughts, and I looked up the passage in my Bible.

> O LORD, you have examined my heart
>   and know everything about me.
> You know when I sit down or stand up.
>   You know my thoughts even when I'm far away.
> You see me when I travel
>   and when I rest at home.
>   You know everything I do.
> You know what I am going to say
>   even before I say it, LORD.
> You go before me and follow me.
>   You place your hand of blessing on my head.
> Such knowledge is too wonderful for me,
>   too great for me to understand!
>
> I can never escape from your Spirit!
>   I can never get away from your presence! (vv. 1–7)

These verses magnify the omnipresence of God in our lives and serve as a sweet reminder that He knows us more deeply than anyone—even our former spouse—and we are never truly alone.

A marriage is defined in Scripture as two people becoming one flesh (see Matt. 19:5 NIV). I read in a book recently that, as a result of this covenant, when divorce happens, it often feels like an amputation without anesthetic.[7] Part of us is gone. Cut off. And it hurts. The longing for intimacy, comfort, and companionship doesn't go away just because our spouse did, so there is a void—an empty space where someone should still be. Psalm 139 reminds us that whether we are married, divorced, or single, God is the One who is always by our side. He is the One who knows us more intimately than any human ever could. The only One who is fully capable of giving us comfort.

But even knowing God is with us, we may still hate the fact that we are alone, and that is exactly when anger at God might try to squirm its way back into our hearts. Countless women have shared with me that even though they believe what the Bible says about God's consistent presence in our lives, their hearts still ache for a companion, and the secret fear of being alone forever is always present. Only God knows if or when He will bring someone new into our lives. So if we long to break free of that nagging fear and have peace with whatever the future brings, we simply have to trust that He knows what is best for us, that He always has a plan, and that He wants us to be joyful and happy. In fact, the word *joy* and related words occur about four hundred times in the Bible, so joy is clearly important to Him! Trust that He has your future in His hands and that He hears the silent cries of your heart.

We can use alone time as a catalyst to build our relationship with God and learn to love ourselves again.

The angry thoughts and questions I struggled with for so long, which I shared in chapter 1, are probably questions every woman has had at one time or another. But unfortunately, these thoughts often make us feel as if our faith is too small and we're being ungrateful for God's promise of His presence. Or we may feel thankful for this spiritual promise, but we'd be even more grateful if we had someone to hold us physically, if God would restore our marriage or answer our other prayers. As a fellow believer who has dealt with this, I want you to know that struggling with loneliness or anger about what happened does not mean we are unspiritual or unfaithful. It simply means we're normal and we're human.

In fact, the Psalms point to the fact that even King David felt lonely quite often. He was a true believer, yet still felt forgotten and forsaken. But his loneliness was exactly what drove him to lean into God even harder. He was a warrior on the battlefield and also a warrior for his faith.

In Psalm 25 King David said, "Turn to me and have mercy, for I am alone and in deep distress. My problems go from bad to worse. Oh, save me from them all!" (vv. 16–17). That sounds exactly like one of the countless pleas to God that have passed through my lips. Then he said, "Feel my pain and see my trouble. Forgive all my sins. See how many enemies I have and how viciously they hate me!" (vv. 18–19). King David was clearly upset. Life had not turned out the way he wanted, and he was battling a deep sense of loneliness, along with frustration that God appeared to be ignoring his pleas for intervention.

But instead of staying upset with God, his prayer took a sudden twist. I wonder if he paused, shoulders slumped, breathing out a heavy sigh as he uttered, "Protect me! Rescue my life from them! Do not let me be disgraced, for in you I take refuge. May integrity and honesty protect me, for I put my hope in you" (vv. 20–21). King David turned to the Lord instead of against Him, even though his trials were many and his faith had been tested. He stopped focusing on the problems and how he didn't have the power to fix everything. Then he placed all his hope in the Lord. This passage teaches us to seek the Lord in even the hardest of times and trust that He is near. Let's allow our troubles to turn us toward God instead of away from Him.

Seasons of feeling alone are the perfect time to focus on our relationship with God and find comfort and contentment in His presence, even if no one else is physically present with us. This was a hard lesson for me to learn and live out. It may not be easy for you either, friend. But over time, as I asked God to make me aware of His presence, to work in my life, and to help me continually transform my thought patterns to focus on the good in life instead of the bad, I began to not only see His interventions but also feel His Spirit no matter where I was or what I was doing.

Gradually, over many months, I began to realize being alone really wasn't that bad after all. In fact, there were a lot of positive aspects. One being, we can use alone time as a catalyst to build our relationship with God and learn to love ourselves again.

Happiness Prompters

- Think of something you like to do in your alone time—read a book, pray, listen to an encouraging podcast, do a craft or project—and make doing that a priority this week.

- Think about all the people you would like to spend more time with over the coming year, and make a point to plan outings or visits with them.

Healing Steps

1. Think of your favorite restaurant or a spot on the beach, at the lake, or in the city that makes you feel at peace. Go there alone and enjoy the solitude.

2. Take yourself out to eat, and step out of your comfort zone to talk with someone new.

3. Reflect on who God is in your life and on your relationship with Him. Read Psalm 25 again, and repeat King David's words in your own prayers. Let God's peace sink into your heart.

Caring for You

Make a playlist of your favorite songs that empower you, lift your spirits, pull you into worship, encourage you, or infuse joy into your heart. Listen to them frequently, and consider having a one-woman sing-along dance party!

Chapter 5

Making the Most of Your Singleness

After a divorce, some of us don't really know how to be alone because we never have been. Being with someone or being someone's spouse may be all we know. It's been so long since we spent time alone that being with the wrong person is almost easier than being by ourselves. No matter how bad the broken relationship was, we might long to still be with our ex because at least that would mean we weren't alone. But it is possible to claim victory over loneliness and there are three important steps to doing this:

1. Recognize it is there and it's normal.
2. Look for positive aspects of being alone.
3. Seek out ways to fill your time with things you enjoy.

We can always determine to make the best of being alone rather than letting being alone steal the best of us, and sometimes the benefits of being alone are overlooked, but they do exist. Let's take a moment to highlight just a few of the benefits of alone time and the ways to fill our time wisely to avoid the threat of loneliness.

Become a Proud, Independent Woman

When I was newly divorced, I was so worried about every decision I had to make that I had a difficult time making any decisions at all, especially when it came to finances, taxes, insurance, and mortgage decisions, which I had never had to deal with before. But as more decision-making became mandatory and I was able to figure things out and manage my household and my life, I grew to enjoy that newfound wisdom, freedom, and independence.

Admittedly, there were days I wanted to crawl under a rock and ignore all the overwhelming responsibilities I was now burdened with. At times the learning curve of all that had to be managed seemed insurmountable. I had to figure out what bills had to be paid and when and how to log in to all the online accounts, handle my taxes for the first time, deal with college tuition and financial aid, buy a car for the first time alone, search for affordable car and health insurance policies, and so much more.

Yet over time I learned so much. I figured things out. I worked things out. All by myself. Inch by inch I began to feel empowered in my decision-making skills and proud of the outcomes I was seeing. I realized I could do this, with God by my side, and discovered I was actually capable of doing things on my own.

Perseverance pushes us further in our journey and helps us learn to be sure of ourselves again.

> We can always determine to make the best of being alone rather than letting being alone steal the best of us.

In time, I learned to enjoy the fact that I was able to decide how I wanted to live my life. I could choose what I wanted to do each day and who I wanted to hang out with without asking for permission or feeling guilty for going out. I could make decisions based on what *I* thought was best for my family and me. I could watch my favorite television programs and movies, attend family gatherings as often as I wanted to, redecorate my home my way, ignore house cleaning until I felt like doing it, and travel wherever and whenever I wanted to go. These were seemingly small, insignificant things, but each step helped me embrace my new freedom. I realized I could stand on my own two feet after all and that the only One I should depend on was God. Over time my confidence grew, which was a major turning point in my healing process.

Eventually I came to recognize I had always been more of a follower in my marriage, submissive to an unhealthy level, passive, and lacking faith in my self-worth and abilities. Like many women, I lived completely unaware of many financial aspects of our life together. I also realized how much of myself I had given up while trying to hang on to a marriage in which I always felt replaceable, unloved, and unappreciated but too scared of being alone and being a single mom to leave. Although making the decision to end the marriage was beyond difficult, it helped me save myself and rediscover who I really was in this world and in God's eyes.

Today I am much more of a decisive, confident, and independent woman than I ever was before, and being single helped me accomplish that. Although I will always wish my story had turned out differently, I am thankful for how God has grown me through this hardship and for how much I have learned. I now own my own home, pay bills, have a successful career, juggle all my responsibilities, have an active social life, and enjoy a wonderful relationship with my children as a single mom. I have finally accepted the truth that I will be okay and I alone am in charge of my life and my happiness.

This quote from Dr. Seuss sums up this truth perfectly: "You have brains in your head. You have feet in your shoes. You can steer yourself any direction you choose. You're on your own. And you know what you know. And *YOU* are the one who'll decide where to go."[1] You are holding the steering wheel of your life. Be proud of who you are and confident in how God has equipped you to handle it. Take control of your life, and start living it instead of just surviving it. You can do this, and you will get through this one day at a time.

I am in charge of my life, and you are in charge of yours now too. Your life and your happiness are in your hands. Take the reins.

Find Ways to Be Creative

I, clearly, love to write. I can spend hours writing chapters, devotions, or blog posts or just typing in my journal. I love creating graphics for social media and engaging with people online. I enjoy cooking new recipes and appetizers (even if just for one!), plus decorating my home and planting new flowers in my deck planters each change of season. I get excited about buying old furniture from antique shops or junkyards and refinishing it to create a beautiful new work of art. I'll even sit down and color if someone gives me a coloring book and crayons.

Another friend took up painting during her season of separation, which brought her new focus and purpose, not to speak of a lot of beautiful paintings to give away to friends and hang in her home as memories of her healing process. Doing something with our hands and being able to see something beautiful develop is always a spirit lifter—as well as a time filler.

My sweet mother, Barbara, went through a painful divorce from my dad when I was in high school. She had always been a talented artist and loved to draw and paint. But after my dad left, she struggled financially as a single mom. She turned her art hobby into a business and became a professional artist, even earning national awards from well-known organizations. But she still enjoyed painting for fun and felt blessed to give her beautiful paintings to friends and family.

Since money is always tight for Malinda, she enjoys doing simple things such as visiting her mom, watching movie marathons, or doing crafts. Whatever outlet we choose, creativity helps us stop focusing on our worries and problems and start using our brains for something fun or productive.

Step Outside Your Comfort Zone and Do Things Alone

Sometimes the only company we really need is our own. My dinner in Florida after my girls left for their trip was the first of many dining experiences I would have alone. But over time I began to enjoy those outings. I could read a good book, talk to a stranger, or just sit and people-watch. Maybe you enjoy going to the movies. Go by yourself. Maybe you enjoy concerts. Go by yourself. Maybe you love shopping. Go to the mall by yourself. Don't be afraid to talk to someone you don't know. Chances are you'll encounter friendly people who make your day or you'll see other people alone who would love to make a new friend. Just as you won't judge them, don't worry about them judging you.

Get a Four-Legged Friend

Although I've never been a pet owner and choose not to take on that kind of responsibility and time commitment, pets can be awesome companions and a sure cure for loneliness. So many women benefit from picking out a furry friend to fill the void of an empty house. Visit a rescue center or animal shelter, and find a dog or cat who could use a friend as much as you could.

Focus on Serving Others

Nothing takes our attention off our problems like focusing on the needs of others. Seek out opportunities to volunteer at a local charitable organization or a special event. Volunteer to lead a Bible study at church or a book study in your neighborhood. Ask your church leadership whether there is a place in the church short of help or if they know an elderly person who needs to know he or she is not forgotten. Contact nursing homes, children's cancer centers, women's shelters, women's prisons, crisis pregnancy centers, or animal shelters, where you can share love and kindness.

An added benefit of volunteer service, in addition to filling up lonely times, is that being around other people who are struggling in different ways not only helps us see our blessings more vividly than our losses but can also lead to the discovery of strengths, gifts, callings, and passions we may have never noticed before. This serves to open even more doors for new adventures and may even spark new purpose for our lives.

Make New Friends

In my early days of singleness, I joined a variety of local meetup groups (www.meetup.com) so I could meet other single people. At first it was awkward showing up to random social events where I faced the choice of mingling with total strangers or standing there all alone. I went to dinners, attended concerts, and even tried mountain hiking, making many new friends at each outing. In addition to the benefit of new relationships, forcing myself to get out there and socialize again helped restore my confidence and courage to be me.

But maybe you're thinking, *I'm just not ready to socialize.* That's perfectly understandable, but sweet friend, you still need some kind of support from others. If you're not quite ready for the social step, a great idea is to join an in-person support group of people who get you and are walking the same hard road as you, and in time those people will likely become friends by virtue of having so much in common. Consider reaching out to women in your community or friends or acquaintances who have experienced separation and divorce and simply setting a time to get together for coffee and conversation. You might also research churches in your area to find programs that help people cope with divorce in a faith-based way.

I realize, regardless of how you go about it, making new friends as an adult is hard work. Especially when we may be feeling less than confident about ourselves due to what we're going through. It's not always fun and can even seem intimidating to put ourselves out there and feel vulnerable. But the benefits of taking that leap of faith and getting out of our comfort zones are priceless.

The key is this: no matter what avenue you choose, keep showing up, and showing up, and showing up again. Commit to showing up to your support group every week or to accepting or initiating social outings. Set your mind on doing something new at least every couple of weeks. You never know who you might randomly meet—until you try. Nothing in life is worthwhile if it doesn't involve some type of risk. Take the risk. Reap the benefits. Enjoy the friends.

Start Something New

Ever dreamed of launching a ministry, starting a blog, or getting a professional license? Do it! Want to begin a new diet and exercise program and get back in shape? Do it! Think you'd love skydiving or learning to drive a boat? Do it! Want to go back to school and get the degree that will open new doors of opportunity? Do it, regardless of what age you are! You know all those things you've always wanted to do? You should go do them!

What is holding you back from doing that one thing—or those many things—you've always thought about doing? I picked up playing golf (and I'm better at it than I thought I could be!), and I picked up snow skiing (and I'm worse at it than I thought I could be!). In any case, post-divorce is the perfect time to do those things you've always wanted to do, feared doing, were discouraged from doing by your former spouse, or lacked the determination to try. Ask God to help you push past your doubts, fears, and insecurities and step outside your comfort zone. Just. Do. It.

Pick Up Something Old

No matter how compatible couples may seem in the beginning, over time we all have to make sacrifices for our spouses. This often means we put aside something we loved for the sake of the relationship. For example, maybe you are a social butterfly, but your former spouse was a homebody, so you stayed home most of the time, or maybe you love hiking, but he preferred biking. Perhaps you've always enjoyed the beach, but your ex-husband longed for the mountains, so you spent most vacations in the high country instead of by the shore.

Think about the hobbies and interests you had before you married and what you may have deferred for your marriage. Allowing yourself to pick up old interests again is a step toward rebuilding yourself and your life and rediscovering who you are.

Find a Face-to-Face Community

Women need other women because God created us for companionship, which is why one of the worst things we can do is isolate ourselves. Although we might feel as if we don't want to be around people or that we're not ready to socialize, as I mentioned earlier, it's so important to surround ourselves with a support system of family and friends and let other people in to encourage us. No matter what avenue you choose for finding community, being around other people is vital to surviving separation and divorce and thriving along the way.

My friend Kristen beamed at how lucky she felt for being connected with the ladies of her Bible study in the beginning of her journey. The ladies took turns organizing weekly girls' nights, such as dinner or shopping, to help her stay busy and prevent isolation. Kristen said, "It was nice to make plans with someone else and get out of the house and do something fun. I wanted to isolate, but people invited me to get out, and they were willing to listen to me and my pain."

Another friend shared how she decided to organize a block party in her neighborhood—where she knew no one. She posted about the event online and was shocked at how many people showed up. People who have now become sweet friends. She shared that her strategy was to always put herself out there no matter what the cultural norms were or what people might think, because you never know what the benefits might be. I bet there are women in your area wishing a woman of courage would open a door for women to gather and build community. Might that woman be you?

Join an Online Support Group

Linda said, "The best thing I've done is to join communities that help me feel connected, such as church small groups, gym accountability partners, online support groups, and caring friends and family." I too found value in all these things but can personally attest to how much of a difference online support groups can make, especially ones whose purposes align with what we are walking through. They may feel impersonal at first, but beautiful friendships can form online with people you may never have met otherwise.

For example, I host a Love Life Again Facebook group that was founded after my last book, *Love Life Again: Finding Joy When Life Is Hard*, was published. I stand amazed at how women from all over the world have fostered beautiful friendships and given endless support and encouragement to one another as they deal with divorce and many other life challenges. All the members needed to know they weren't alone. In this group, they found people who understood them and cared for them. It's become a place where they feel safe to share their feelings and struggles. (Feel free to join me in that

Facebook group, if you'd like, or connect with me on my Facebook author page!) There are countless support groups on Facebook and online for women facing the end of their marriage. It just takes a little research and effort to find them. Real community and friendships can happen thanks to modern technology. Take advantage of it.

Be Good to Yourself

Even though time to ourselves is often hard to find, especially when young children are in the home or a job keeps us stretched for time, it is critical for our well-being and our healing. Maybe it's been a while since you focused on yourself. If so, now is the time to start.

> *Take control of your life, and start living it instead of just surviving it.*

Think of things that bring you delight and happiness; then make a commitment to yourself to do at least one of those things consistently. Maybe you love long walks in the park, bubble baths with a glass of wine and a magazine, yoga, hiking, horseback riding, or driving through the countryside with the windows rolled down. Perhaps you need to hire a babysitter for just a few hours—or call on a loved one to help—to give you a couple of hours of "me time." Maybe there is a hobby you used to enjoy before children or marriage; why not pick that hobby up again? Maybe your heart would lighten if you began seeing a counselor each week and talking about your feelings in a safe place. Choose things that will promote your well-being, and don't let any destructive habits creep in.

Think about what would make you feel better about yourself. Maybe it's a makeover, a trendy new haircut, or starting a diet and exercise program. Go shopping and update your wardrobe. If money is tight, visit your local Goodwill store. It's amazing what incredible name-brand clothing you can find! If nothing is holding you back, consider moving to a new city for a fresh start, signing up for an overseas mission trip, or simply finding a new church that welcomes you with love and open arms.

Whatever you think of, if it will bring you refreshment and enjoyment, make time for it. Then make it part of your weekly or monthly routine. Don't feel guilty for making yourself a priority. You deserve it and owe it to yourself to take care of yourself.

Create a Self-Discipline of Gratefulness

It's not happy people who are thankful; it's thankful people who are happy. We've all walked a hard road, no matter our situation, and many of us are still walking it today. But one thing we can all do to change our hearts, even in the brokenness of our lives, is maintain an attitude of thankfulness. It's a great practice but can be hard, especially when so many things are weighing on our hearts and countless problems may seem insurmountable.

No matter what is going on around us, we are in control of what goes on within us. Having an intentional attitude of gratitude, rather than obsessing over our losses, helps us stay focused on what we do have. Gratitude compels us to focus on God's goodness rather than the prayers that still seem unanswered. When we stop complaining about all the troubles we have and become thankful for the blessings we have, our perspective will begin to change.

Consider creating a gratitude journal in which you record all the big and little blessings God bestows on you during this season. Or create a blessings jar, and each time something good happens or you feel God has blessed you in a certain way, write that down on a little piece of paper and put it in the jar. As you see this jar filling up, I promise it will lift your spirits and help you continue to focus on thankfulness, as well as serve as a daily reminder of all the little things God is doing for you that you might have forgotten or overlooked otherwise.

Either of these options will help you stay acutely aware of the fact that God is at work in your life and staying close by your side. And months down the road, you'll have either a journal packed with precious memories of God's goodness and faithfulness or a jar full of blessings to remember! It doesn't matter how you choose to make gratefulness a habitual pattern of thinking. All that matters is that you do it!

Living with a mind-set of gratitude prepares the soil where true happiness will blossom.

Set Some Goals

During my many years in the corporate world before transitioning to Christian speaking and writing and being a stay-at-home mom, I spent a lot of time setting goals for performance and success. I was required to strive for those goals and was evaluated based on them when performance review time rolled around. I saw the value in this process, and it became an invaluable skill I've used in many areas of life—especially in navigating the rocky waters of my new normal.

After divorce, especially when your spouse has walked away and left you to handle everything you never had to deal with before, getting everything done can be scary and overwhelming. So overwhelming that you feel paralyzed and don't know what to tackle first. On one of the many days when my head was spinning because of all the new responsibilities I was trying to juggle, I decided to sit down and write out some goals.

I wrote out goals for how to manage my finances, pay off debt, and repair my credit, which had taken a major blow during separation due to circumstances beyond my control. But I also wrote out some personal goals for myself. Projects I wanted to tackle. Things I wanted to learn or try. Hobbies I might like to pick up. Ways to improve myself and my attitude. And so on.

Setting personal goals can help us start dreaming about the future instead of obsessing over the past. We can't change the past, but the future is a blank canvas, and we are holding the paintbrush. Set small goals, and keep track of your progress so you can stay motivated along the way, but don't be afraid to set big goals as well. In fact, set such a big goal for yourself that you'll be blown away and thrilled when you accomplish it! But if you can't do anything else, set a simple goal for tomorrow. Plan to wake up, smile, and tell yourself it's going to be a good day.

Last but certainly not least …

Invest in Rediscovering Yourself

Being alone isn't the worst thing in the world, and when treated with care and trust in God, it can propel you toward the day when you will wake up and realize you have changed for the better. You'll see the results of your willingness to put in the effort to create the kind of life you longed for and become who you wanted to be.

You'll feel empowered, stronger, and more confident. You'll have picked up new hobbies, made new friends, learned new things, and enjoyed new activities. You'll feel a renewed sense of happiness and contentment in the life God has you living. And maybe, for the first time in a long time, as you look at yourself in the mirror, you'll proudly view the reflection of the amazing woman you really are and see with your own eyes how far you've really come.

Maybe it's been a while since you focused on yourself. If so, now is the time to start.

As for me, the time came when I knew that I needed to learn to just be Tracie and that being alone was the perfect time to find myself again. A time to be me, not just someone's wife or mother. Not just someone who put everyone's needs and desires first while pushing hers to the back burner, if not forgetting them completely. Not just someone who felt unworthy and never enough. Not just the insecure single person in a circle of married couples. Not just the woman labeled by divorce. Not just someone trying to survive and get through another day, but someone amazing and happy who had recovered from her heartbreak.

I wanted to learn to be *just me* again. That is my hope for you as well. You can use this alone time to rediscover yourself. Rediscover the woman who has her whole life ahead of her, deserves to be loved by someone who loves her with his whole heart, and is the

confident woman God created her to be. A woman who may wish
her story had turned out differently but chooses to enjoy the life she
is living no matter what it looks like. A proud, confident woman
who can wake up each morning with peace in her heart and a smile
on her face.

I was so ready to be that girl, and I bet you are too.

Optimism Is a State of Mind

Thinking back to that trip with my daughters helps me remember
how God showed up to start the process of healing my heart and
helping me overcome the sadness of loneliness. As I sat on the
plane on the way home from Florida, I accepted that I didn't have
to feel lonely along the way, even though I had no idea how long I
might be physically alone. Maybe God would bring someone new
into my life, or maybe He wouldn't. Maybe it would be next year
or ten years from now. Maybe never. There was no way to know
for sure. However, what I did know for sure was that, either way,
I would be okay. I could be happy. And I had to trust God with
my future.

Loneliness is a state of mind, not a state of being, and optimism
about our situation can be our state of mind if we practice it on a
daily basis. Friend, you hold the power to overcome loneliness and
feelings of isolation. You can focus on and obsess over being lonely
or commit to making the most of your time, rediscovering yourself, growing closer to God, taking up new hobbies, spending more
time with friends and family, and making decisions independently.
You can focus on being lonely or develop new skills and even build
a new career for yourself. You can focus on being lonely or take

advantage of every opportunity to seek out and organize time with friends and family.

I determined to face my loneliness head on and started living life differently. After slowly implementing all these tips, I began reinventing my life and rediscovering who I am.

> *Be that woman who may wish her story had turned out differently but chooses to enjoy the life she is living no matter what it looks like.*

Just as God had whispered to my heart, I eventually grew to understand and accept that my divorce was indeed not the end of me, and your divorce is not the end of you either! In fact, it's only the beginning. A new beginning with God by your side. The beginning of something good. Actually, it's the beginning of something even better than you could ever imagine even if you didn't want a new beginning. Life can be good and wonderful again, and so can you. Commit to taking a stand, holding your head high, and stepping into a new version of yourself. Imagine who you want to be and how you want to feel and live. Then imagine having the courage to bring that version of yourself to life.

This may not be the life we thought we would have, but it is the life we have now. You and I are still breathing. We have the gift of life, and we still have a future. We can let life's hardships steal the best of us, or we can make the best of the life we've been given.

Happiness Prompters

- Make a list of things you like about yourself. Then, ask three people who know and love you how they would describe you. Have them share everything they love about you, and let their words serve as reassurance of who you are and the quality you bring to their lives.

- Create a self-esteem folder. Include your own list and also record each of the kind things your three people said about you on a piece of paper and put it in this folder. Anytime someone compliments you, write it down and file it away. On those days when you feel like you have no good qualities, pull out your self-esteem folder and remind yourself that you are a wonderful you.

Healing Steps

1. Consider this chapter's suggestions for how to overcome lone-liness. Prioritize them in order of things you want to do, with 1 being the most important to you right now and 16 being the least important.

___ Become a proud, independent woman.

___ Find ways to be creative.

___ Step outside your comfort zone and do things alone.

___ Get a four-legged friend.

___ Focus on serving others.

___ Join a faith-based, church-sponsored divorce support group.

___ Research community support groups for separated and divorced people, and join one.

___ Make new friends.

___ Start something new.

___ Pick up something old.

___ Find a face-to-face community.

___ Join an online support group.

___ Be good to yourself.

___ Create a self-discipline of gratefulness.

___ Set some goals.

___ Invest in rediscovering yourself.

2. Pick the five highest-ranking activities above, and write them in your journal in order of importance. Then circle or highlight at least two of those ideas you can begin implementing this week. Consider what is needed to start striving toward these things.

3. Over the next few months, revisit your list and record the good things that happened when you stepped outside your comfort zone. Pick one or two more activities you could begin to further promote emotional healing.

Caring for You

Think of something fun you've always wanted to do or used to enjoy doing. Invite a friend to do it with you and hold you accountable for following through.

Chapter 6

Breaking the Power of Shame

Years ago, I took my children to Carowinds, a large local theme park. I committed to myself to not focus on the blistering summer heat and just be excited to spend the day with them. Everything was fun and giggles until about an hour into our outing when they asked me to ride the new roller coaster with them.

I stared at the massive rails looming high in the sky. Screaming passengers whizzed by and my heart began to race. I was torn. I didn't want my kids to ride alone—I probably would have worried myself to pieces until they got off—but nothing in my soul wanted to get on that contraption. Why would I want to buckle myself into a seat, go a million miles an hour upside down, get bounced around like a ball tied to a paddle board, and likely have the living daylights scared out of me?

After a few minutes of trying to convince them to do another ride, my mom sense overrode my common sense and I agreed to ride along. After a torturous, anxiety-ridden, hot, and long wait in line, we finally boarded the train car, strapped ourselves in, and waited to pull out of the station. *Clickety-clackety, clickety-clackety, clickety-clackety* filled the air as we inched up to the highest part of the track. My heart was racing, and I was beating myself up inside for agreeing to this nonsense. And did I mention I also have a fear of heights? Mercy.

We reached the peak, and the train car plummeted downhill at warp speed. I could see the huge loop of track looming ahead, which would soon hang me upside down as the cars roared around the circle. My stomach leaped into my throat, and my immediate instinct was to close my eyes as tight as they would shut.

My eyes did not open until I heard the slow *clickety-clack* once again, serving as proof that this horrific ride was almost over and I was nearly back in the station, safe on stable land.

I know a lot of people love roller coasters, but clearly, I'm not one of them. My coping method for dealing with this undesirable situation was to try to pretend it wasn't happening while refusing to look at what was ahead of me. I ignored my emotions and didn't listen to the warning alarms going off in my head and instead let the roller coaster jerk me back and forth at its discretion. Trust me—I did not enjoy it. Not even a little bit. I vowed to never get on one again and have held firm to that vow.

As I recalled this scenario, I couldn't help but consider how similar it was to the roller coaster of life I found myself on after my marriage ended. Plummeting downhill into scary and unknown territory, feeling trapped and helpless to escape. My heart was shattered and my mind exhausted from the storm raging in me and around me. I wanted to close my eyes and pretend none of it was happening. I wanted to ignore the twists and turns that lay ahead. I longed for just one day of escape from dealing with insurmountable problems and joy-robbing emotions.

Yet on the other hand, I wanted to speed ahead and wake up in a whole new place, having left the nightmare behind, having overcome the pain, and feeling healed, whole, and happy again. A place where the worst had passed and the train had pulled up into a new station of life.

But I avoided dealing with my roller coaster of emotions and let them get the best of me. I felt strapped into a life of sorrow and incapable of feeling normal again. Stuck in the pain and drowning in oceans of negative thoughts, all of which were stealing my happiness and my ability to start moving forward in a positive direction.

A Roller Coaster of Emotions

When a marriage fails—no matter whose fault it was or what the circumstances were and even if you wanted the marriage to be over—a wide range of emotions flood your heart and keep your mind in constant turmoil.

One day we're thankful for our newfound freedom, and the next day we're lonely and wishing we still had a spouse at home. One day we feel relieved to be out of an unhappy marriage, and the next day we're wishing things hadn't ended. One day we are incredibly angry at our ex for what he may have done to us, and the next day we're feeling like we still love him, feel sorry for him, and miss him. One day we feel happy; the next day we're heavy with sadness. One day we feel good about ourselves; the next day we feel like the most worthless person in the world. One day we think we're getting things figured out; the next day a new problem hits and fear starts making it hard to breathe again. One day we are trying to hold our heads high; the next day we feel shame and embarrassment creeping back in. Strides forward, then leaps backward, can easily feel like the pattern of our lives.

The first six months of separation are probably the hardest part of the journey because emotions run rampant. An article from a divorce website states that during this period "women are more prone to symptoms of depression, poor health, loneliness, work inefficiency, insomnia, memory difficulties, and increased substance abuse."[1]

As women, we tend to feel more helpless and vulnerable than men do in this situation because we may have been financially dependent on our husbands, even if we had a job outside the home. We may feel incompetent to deal with the finances, which serves to further damage our self-confidence. Some women were the ones who handled all the finances in their marriages, but I would venture to say a large majority of women left it up to their husbands, only to get blindsided when their marriages ended, especially if the spouses walked away and abandoned all responsibilities.

The longer we were married, the more intense the roller coaster of emotions will be when our marriage falls apart, but it's important to intentionally deal with them so they don't wreak havoc on our hearts, minds, and bodies. Emotions are powerful. They determine our moods, how we interact with others, how we handle problems, and more. If we want to be mentally stronger and have more confidence, we first have to recognize what's going on inside us. If we ignore or suppress any of these emotions, they're likely to get worse over time instead of better. Even when we are longing to heal, move forward, and enjoy the life we have, emotions can be a major stumbling block if ignored—with shame and guilt at the top of the list.

I eventually realized that the longer I let my emotions overwhelm me and the longer I let shame and guilt hold my heart and happiness hostage, the longer I was going to stay stuck doing the unhappiness limbo. Either I could keep letting those feelings dictate how I lived each day or I could stand tall, pick myself up, take control of my thoughts, and choose to deal with my emotions head on—with eyes wide open.

For true healing to begin, we must recognize how we are feeling and thinking and be aware of the impact those thoughts and feelings have on us and our future. And not only recognize them for what they are but also deal with them.

> The best weight we can ever lose is the weight of other people's opinions.

Shame Has No Place in Your Heart

One of the first things I did as a volunteer for Proverbs 31 Ministries more than fifteen years ago was to write for the free daily devotional, "Encouragement for Today," which now reaches more than one million women and men each day with God's Word. I am confident God called me to be transparent in my writing and speaking over the years at Proverbs 31. At times I've felt that was a curse instead of a call, because who wants to constantly share the ugly parts of her life? But I've learned that doing so helps women connect with me emotionally and opens up the possibility for God to speak to their hearts and change their lives. I feel immensely blessed when I see God use my pain for a purpose.

However, when my marriage imploded, it was a whole different ball game.

When I was dealing with all the new struggles separation brought, the devotional ideas God laid on my heart obviously stemmed from what He was teaching me about His faithfulness during that time. But instead of being transparent, I wanted to hide my ugliness and the messiness of my life from everyone. I put a lot of effort into wording my monthly devotions to deliver the truth of God's goodness while only hinting about my current problems rather than being open about them. I would use phrases like "difficult situation" or "painful season," yet never shared clear, vulnerable details about my broken marriage. My writing still communicated God's truth but was void of any transparency that might lead someone to figure out what was actually going on in my life.

Why, you ask? I was ashamed. So crushingly embarrassed and ashamed.

> Let shame go, and let God's love and acceptance in.

I was ashamed for women to know I was separated and headed for divorce. I was embarrassed my husband left me for someone else. I was ashamed that, as a Christian, a speaker, and a writer, I was now going to be a divorce statistic. I was ashamed people might think I wasn't capable of keeping my husband happy. I was ashamed people might secretly feel I wasn't enough—as a woman, wife, friend, lover, cook, housekeeper, mom. Or maybe they would wonder what actually happened and start thinking I had done something terribly wrong because they didn't know the facts.

Nobody but me knew the painful details of our situation, so I was convinced I would be judged. I was afraid of no longer being accepted or respected as a woman of God, much less a public speaker and author. I worried I'd have to give up the career I'd spent my life building. Shame seemed to overtake my soul.

In fact, I was so ashamed that although my husband left in October 2015, the first time I shared honestly about my separation with my public audience was in January 2017 on my blog (www. traciemiles.com). It was a rather long post, but below are a few key paragraphs:

January 23, 2017

Why I Would Treasure Your Prayers for 2017

I don't think I've ever been so glad to put a year behind me and begin a brand new year full of fresh hopes and dreams. And I'll tell you why....

During the past year—which honestly has felt much like a disaster— my family and I have endured the most difficult, heartbreaking, and horrific storm we've ever had to go through. Fifteen months ago, my husband of more than twenty-five years decided to walk away from our marriage and our family. Throughout this trial, I have tried to wear a smile and stay positive, stand firm in my faith, live life as normally as possible, be strong for my children, and continue in ministry. But I have to admit there have been times when the burden felt too heavy to bear and an overwhelming deluge of emotions seemed to be controlling my mind and my life....

I would have done anything in the world to avoid this happening. However, I've finally come to realize through a lot of prayer, faith, and emotional and spiritual healing, that sometimes, no matter how badly we want something, strive for it, or pray for it, it may not work out the way we wanted or prayed for. All we can do when this happens is commit to trust God's ways, even if we don't understand them or like them, and believe He has an even better plan full of joy and happiness and blessing in store for us. And that is where I find myself today.

I loved my husband dearly, and have always prayed fervently for him and our marriage. Over the past year, I prayed endlessly for a change in his heart and mind, and even prayed for some type of miraculous restoration to occur if that was God's will. However, at this point, it seems clear that restoration does not appear to be in God's plan for us....

I must confess that sharing this raw emotional wound and deeply personal situation publicly sort of feels like standing in front of a huge firing squad with a blindfold on and then giving the signal to fire. But rather than live in fear of judgment or opinions from potentially well-meaning people who don't have a full understanding of our situation, or worry and fret over what certain people might think or say, I had to follow the nudging of the Holy Spirit and be humble and honest, while choosing to place my fears in God's hands and trust He will protect my heart and my children's hearts.

As if it were yesterday, I remember breaking into a full sweat when I hit the Post button and watched my most shameful secret go public on the home page of my blog. My heart raced, and a knot formed in my stomach. I lost many hours of sleep that night as I tossed and turned in anticipation of reading the comments the following day.

Rather than trusting that God's favor and protection would fall on my obedience and that He had a purpose for my pain, I was prepared for the worst and wasn't sure my heart could take it. I was convinced I would get lambasted in the comment section for choosing to go through with divorce. I was sure women would leave hateful or critical comments scorning me as a person and lecturing me, albeit with good intention, about the importance of the covenant of marriage and how we are called to forgive and reconcile at all costs.

Feelings of failure and embarrassment can be a tool the enemy uses to keep us suffering in silence.

Yet what happened was exactly the opposite. Dozens upon dozens of comments were posted, each one filled with life-giving words and unwavering compassion that brought me to my knees. Beautiful encouragement. Bible verses to hold me up. Reminders of God's grace, mercy, and goodness. Precious prayers. Countless women meekly uttering "Me too." Some women even emailed me to share how much their hearts ached for me and how closely they could relate to what I was going through. I sat and stared at my computer screen with tears of relief and joy sliding down my cheeks.

They didn't judge me. They loved me. They were looking for hope and encouragement as well as help for their own hearts to start healing. All those sweet women, most of whom I will never meet in person, helped me realize I didn't have anything to be ashamed of. They wrapped virtual arms around my heart and played a major role in helping me deal with the shame and put it behind me as I was reminded over and over of God's love for me no matter what. There were a few people, of course, who left well-intended judgmental comments and advice for how I should or could be handling things differently, but those comments were few and far between. My heart was so blessed by all the support and encouragement that had already sunk into my soul that the negative comments didn't stick in my insecure mind as they normally would have.

Rather than regretting being vulnerably honest about my situation, I regretted not doing it sooner. As a burden was lifted off my shoulders, I discovered the best weight we can ever lose is the weight of other people's opinions.

I also found myself wondering how much further along I might have been in the healing journey had I asked God sooner for the courage to stop hiding my struggles and be transparent with others. How differently might I have dealt with things if I had opened the door for those who loved me most to walk closer with me when I felt I couldn't take another step? I can't help but wonder if I would have grown and emotionally healed more quickly had the bondage of shame been broken much earlier.

Through all the sweet words of understanding and kindness I received online, I finally accepted that my spouse's decisions and my marital status did not define my value—only God did. My own mistakes and flaws did not determine my value either—only God did. I didn't need to worry about what other people thought because all that mattered was what God said about me and that He loved me unconditionally, whether I was married or not. Romans 5:8 says, "God has shown us how much he loves us—it was while we were still sinners that Christ died for us!" (GNT). We are so loved by Him, and our value is in Him alone, but it's so easy to forget this truth when we feel rejected and betrayed.

> Shame tells us we are guilty; Jesus died on the cross to pronounce us innocent. Shame makes us want to hide; in Christ we are forgiven and free.

It took awhile for me to experience this truth, and maybe you're still struggling to accept it as well. It's challenging not to let shame take up residence in our hearts especially if we've messed up or when someone we loved and trusted has betrayed us. Feelings of failure and embarrassment can be a tool the enemy uses to keep us suffering in silence.

Shame is a major roadblock to happiness, whether we are embarrassed about something a former spouse did or ashamed of our own actions and choices. Shame is a heavy weight to carry. It causes us to harbor negative, self-condemning thoughts that plague our minds every day. It causes us to doubt a holy God could really love us. In shame, we also place self-defeating labels on ourselves, which only makes things worse.

The key to breaking the power of shame is found in Jesus Christ alone. Shame tells us we are guilty; Jesus died on the cross to pronounce us innocent. Shame makes us want to hide; in Christ we are forgiven and free. When we put our trust in Jesus and who we are in

Him, the power of shame can be broken and the power of Jesus can usher in healing and happiness.

Our hearts were meant to be free. Let shame go, and let God's love and acceptance in.

Happiness Prompters

- What is the funniest movie you've ever watched? Find it and watch it! Laughter is the best remedy for a hurting heart. If you don't feel like laughing, then you need to do exactly that.
- Look yourself in the mirror, and tell your reflection that she is amazing—every morning.

Healing Steps

1. What are the thoughts you struggle with that make you feel the most ashamed? Ask for God's forgiveness as well as healing for the deepest wounds in your heart. Each time you think those negative thoughts, stop yourself and remember God's grace and forgiveness are yours.

2. What friends or family members can you be vulnerable with to open the door for more support and encouragement? Have courage, and reach out to those people today.

3. How much lighter and happier do you think you would be if you stopped worrying about what other people are saying or

thinking? Let this thought help you begin to let go of the weight of others' opinions and begin focusing on who God says you are instead.

Caring for You

Forgive yourself today for whatever is poisoning your heart and mind with shame. Be compassionate with yourself. Negative, self-condemning thoughts are an obstacle to self-improvement and healing.

Chapter 7

Releasing the Burden of Guilt

Just as shame has no place in our hearts, neither does guilt. Guilt is to the soul what pain is to the body. It hurts, it keeps us stuck in regret and confusion, and it stands in the way of putting the past behind us and living healthy, happy lives.

I can always second-guess myself and feel guilty about my marriage ending. I could second-guess myself forever, and these types of thoughts are likely ones we all secretly struggle with even if the core reason for the demise of our relationship doesn't lie on our shoulders. Nobody is perfect, and when tragedy strikes in a marriage, we can drive ourselves batty pondering how we failed most.

Maybe your situation is different from mine. Maybe *you* were the cause of your marriage ending. Maybe you fell out of love with your spouse and decided to leave. Maybe you had an affair. Maybe you feel guilty because you wonder whether you did enough to save the marriage or because you did not want to reconcile when things blew up even if your ex did. Maybe you stayed in the marriage way longer than you should have for the sake of the kids, but as it turns out, it was worse for the kids, and now you and your children are paying the emotional and mental consequences. You may be shouldering the burden not only of shame but also of guilt.

Or maybe you have guilt not about the end of the marriage but about what happened afterward. Perhaps you made choices you are not proud of as you tried to wade through the messiness of survival. Some people turn to drinking, drugs, or inappropriate relationships to put a Band-Aid on the loneliness. Or they do things outside of their normal character, maybe even against their beliefs—things they never imagined themselves doing. But this new life is so strange and foreign—marked by a newfound freedom and way too much time—that the door swings open for sin to enter. I certainly have some deep regrets for certain choices I've made in the wasteland of my failed marriage, and maybe you do too.

Guilt is to the soul what pain is to the body.

But guilt can destroy our self-esteem and keep us in a tangled mess. It can prevent us from embracing the life God has us living right now. Guilt-laden thoughts plague our hearts and minds every day, continually whispering we've done something wrong, even if we haven't. Sometimes they convince us we are unforgivable.

Guilt can blind us to God's love, strip us of hope, and paralyze us, robbing us of the strength we need to let go of the past and embrace the future with confidence. Deep down we may feel we don't even deserve happiness, so why try?

When we feel guilty about something, we convince ourselves not only that we did something bad but that we *are* bad. We've likely all done things we wish we hadn't done, especially when we're trying to survive the chaos and confusion of divorce. But our mistakes could never steal our value in God's eyes, and they definitely do not define us.

Jesus gave His life on the cross so we wouldn't have to carry the burden of those regrets forever. According to Psalm 103:12, "He has removed our sins as far from us as the east is from the west." And Romans 8:1 says, "Now there is no condemnation for those who belong to Christ Jesus." Whatever is heavy on your heart, confess it, ask for forgiveness, let it go, and embrace the freedom Christ wants you to have. Give yourself the same empathy, compassion, and forgiveness you would give a friend who messed up in some way. You deserve God's grace, mercy, and forgiveness as much as anyone else, so don't let guilt stand in the way of you accepting those gifts.

I love this quote from a website I recently visited: "Guilt doesn't care whether you twisted over the decision to divorce for weeks, months or even years. Guilt doesn't take into account the amount of courage it may have taken you to finally decide to divorce yourself from a marriage that had already been dead for years. But guilt is not the truth."[1]

Only God's Word is truth. Guilt is not God's will for our lives. It is a tactic the devil uses to keep us from moving forward. It causes us to stay stuck in what happened and incapable of living life to the fullest. Even if we did everything possible to be a loving, faithful wife and mother and prevent divorce, the guilt of divorce still runs deep. We may always wonder, *Did I do enough?* Sometimes the lies of guilt can be our loudest thoughts, especially if we know we've made poor choices.

Numbing Disappointment

Once our divorce was final, I found myself in a horrible place (in case you haven't figured that out yet!) and admittedly did not make the best decisions in my damaged state of mind, much less always choose the best coping mechanisms for my grief. I was lonely, hopeless, and afraid. I wanted to feel better, less alone, and fulfilled. I wanted to feel needed, seen, loved, and prioritized. I needed to feel secure financially. These are all valid, common wants and needs but ones that can lead us into temptation if we're not careful.

My friend Lysa TerKeurst wrote in her book *It's Not Supposed to Be This Way*, "If [the enemy] can isolate us, he can influence us. And his favorite of all entry points is through our disappointments.... The enemy uses disappointments to cause so much trouble in an unsettled heart. A heart hungry for something to ease the ache of disappointment is especially susceptible to the most dangerous forms of desire."[2] If only I had read that warning before I let disappointment take the steering wheel of my life, I could have avoided some of the issues I brought on myself. You see, once I finally accepted the marriage was over for real, although acceptance is a phase we must all get to at some point, disappointment became a weight I couldn't put down. I was no longer the same person mentally or emotionally that I had been before. I was scarred. I was changed. I felt more lost, confused, and alone than ever. This profound, complex disappointment began to drive my thoughts and actions.

For the first year and a half after our separation, emotions ran high for my children and me, and I was so thankful for the support, love, and friendship we all shared. They were the only things in my life that felt right, normal, and good. At the time of separation, my son was still in high school and living at home, so we were together every day, while both my daughters were already in college or beyond. So once my son went off to college, I felt an even larger sense of loneliness due to dealing with empty-nest syndrome all alone, and I had way too much free time on my hands to fill the void.

To mask or numb the loneliness, I often turned to drinking or going to parties with friends, which I rarely did before. I stopped getting together with people I had always spent time with so I could make room for new social activities, plus I didn't feel comfortable going to couples outings anymore even if someone was sweet enough to invite me. I gradually put my Bible reading, quiet time, church-going, and worship songs on the back burner. Less and less were God's truths the founding principles for how I lived my everyday life. I got involved in relationships I knew were not right. I hurt my children with some of my poor decisions and had to carry the burden of their disappointment in me.

For quite some time I just wasn't right. I wasn't myself. I wasn't someone I was proud of anymore. I wasn't someone I loved or even liked. I had new regrets. My self-esteem was already at an all-time low, and when you're making choices you aren't proud of, that damage is only compounded. Some days I didn't even recognize myself in the mirror or like who I saw.

After some time I became aware of how I had changed in many ways, but I didn't know exactly what was happening or why, much less how to fix all my new self-inflicted problems. I felt helpless and hopeless to do a U-turn and get back to who and where I used to be. I also knew that would require more sacrifices of relationships and result in even more hard changes, and I was so tired of sacrifices and changes. I only wanted to be happy, accepted, and loved. My heart was unsettled and opened a crack for the enemy to wiggle in.

I am not proud to admit these details of my journey, and that distressing vision of standing in front of the firing squad is creeping back into my consciousness as I write this, threatening to make me hit the Delete button on all the confessions above. But I never want to come across as holier-than-thou because, girl, that would be far from the truth. Despite being Christian, we are all sinners. No one is completely innocent, so I'm not merely preaching truths I've learned from a book. Instead, I write from experience with the good and not-so-good lessons learned from this journey. So I feel led to share vulnerably here because you may be suffering secretly with some issues as well and I want you to know I can relate to how you feel, what you're going through, and how hard it is to make good decisions in a bad season. We will all make mistakes, big and small, but it's okay.

Everybody Makes Mistakes

During my season of feeling lost, directionless, disappointed, and unhappy with who I had become and how I was living my life, a Scripture verse would repeatedly float through my mind: "I don't really understand myself, for I want to do what is right, but I don't do it. Instead, I do what I hate" (Rom. 7:15). This is where the apostle Paul found himself—so far from who he wanted to be because of sin in his life. He was aware of his daily struggle with sin and that he was frequently tempted to engage in behaviors that weren't right in God's eyes. He knew who he wanted to be, but life and sin kept getting in the way in spite of his pursuit of holiness.

Paul was a real person who experienced many traumatic events. Although his situations were different from ours, the thoughts and emotions were the same. But he was a sinner too, just as we are. All capable of making mistakes and then wishing we hadn't made them, possibly despising what we do but caught up in a cycle of sin. All in need of God's grace and forgiveness. All desperate for rescue from the only One who can rescue us.

I believe many women have struggles similar to Paul's. Women who would do anything to mask the pain, numb the disappointment no matter what it takes, escape the war zone in their lives, and get control of the psychological battlefield in their minds, even if just for a short time. Women who long for someone or something to fill the emptiness in their hearts and will do almost anything to fulfill that desire. Women who acted out of hurt or anger and caused damage in their lives they wish they could undo. I know I am not alone in messing up, and **if you have a few skeletons in your closet from trying to soothe the pain in your heart, you're not alone** either.

I had one friend who opened up to me very vulnerably when she confessed, "I sort of lost my mind after my first divorce. I made so many stupid mistakes and bad decisions." She shared that she was "stupidly promiscuous" after her first divorce. Not just one-night stands, but using sex as a way to keep a man in her life. She was desperately seeking someone or something to validate her and to meet her need to be loved and desired, only to be disappointed every time. As a result, her self-confidence and self-esteem were further damaged, and she sank into depression again. She quickly began dating someone else seriously, which eventually led her into a second marriage. All her bad decisions played a role in the problems with her second husband. And once her second divorce was underway, her life went on a downward spiral. She stopped going to church, the one place she knew she should be.

Holly was diagnosed with post-divorce PTSD by her doctor due to her abusive marriage. Knowing this helped her make sense of all that had happened and opened the door for her to begin healing. However, fear, anxiety, and nightmares constantly plagued her, and the smallest thing could send her over the edge. She struggled with many mental and emotional issues, and food became one of her biggest coping mechanisms. Her ex-husband had been known to withhold funds to purchase food while they were separated, so when food was available, her cravings were uncontrollable. When a situation would trigger an emotion, she would turn to eating in an attempt to numb or avoid her feelings. This clearly affected her physical and emotional health.

Kristen confessed that her anger and bitterness got the best of her after her husband left because her heart had been so hardened by all the hurt and betrayal. Her in-laws' "advice" hurt her deeply, and she felt they blamed her for the end of her marriage. She responded by exploding in hurt and anger and doing and saying things to her former mother-in-law and sister-in-law that she would regret, even though her statements were true. She also started dating quickly and entered into a physical relationship simply because she wanted to find someone, anyone, who would care about her and make her feel loved. But these types of relationships only left her feeling even more confused about her value and her future.

Shelly told me she would go out drinking when her daughter was spending time at her dad's house, because the alcohol helped her loosen up and not be shy and withdrawn around others. She enjoyed laughing, being noticed, and feeling less alone. She pursued men for the wrong reasons and had long relationships, even staying in a very abusive relationship with a boyfriend, expecting these men to complete her. She sacrificed her self-worth, friendships, and family, trying to make the relationships work in attempts to gain the life she thought she so desperately wanted.

I could tell story after story of women who have shared the regrets they now carry because of misguided actions after a painful divorce. But let's get on to the hope and recovery that are possible in Christ! We do not have to live in a pool of regrets, because we are forgiven and it is never too late to turn our lives around.

> Even in the worst of times,
> God is always faithful.

Malinda recognized the problems she created with her decisions, so she took four years off of dating to rediscover herself and get her heart and mind back in the right place after her second failed marriage. She spent significant time in God's Word and in prayer and committed to herself that the only way she would date again is if God clearly sent a man to her. She refuses to be disrespected or used ever again, and she became confident she deserves nothing but true love from a man. She said, "My heavenly Father is the only man in my life besides my sons and grandson. It has taken me sixteen years to love myself again, and no one is taking that away from me again." Amen, sister!

Holly recognized her struggle with food after her divorce and eventually came to the place where she craved healing and wholeness much more than food. She committed to doing the work to process her feelings and recover from the pain that the abuse and divorce had caused her. When she sought God, He met her right where she was. She drew closer to God through prayer, and He opened the door for Christian counseling and wonderful opportunities to get involved in her community, all of which helped her overcome her core issues and start walking a path of recovery.

Kristen knew her way of dealing with her pain and her in-laws was not right. For months she refused to listen to the whisper in her spirit prompting her to turn her anger over to God and to avoid falling prey to offense, arguments, and heated tempers. But the day came when she decided she was going to listen to that voice urging her to be the person God wanted her to be. At times she still struggles with getting into relationships with men, looking for validation and love, but she has learned to be aware when a relationship is not going in a positive direction. Now she can muster the courage to end it, always reminding herself that her value comes from God alone.

Shelly began listening to that inner voice convicting her spirit that she needed to change herself and her lifestyle and that she was the only one who could bring about that change. She finally realized that "Drinking doesn't take away the problems. It was a temporary numbing solution—everything you try to escape is still there, waiting for your sober mind. I finally learned my worth wasn't in anyone else's opinion, only in God's eyes."

In order to bring about the necessary changes, Shelly began to go to Bible study and church, praying more and always listening for

God's voice. She chose godly people to spend time with, and she listened to their wisdom. She walked away from her abusive relationship and stood strong against letting that person back into her life. She also reestablished relationships with family and friends.

Lastly, Shelly confessed that, without God, it is likely she would not be here today to tell her story. While in the abusive relationship with her ex-boyfriend, her life was threatened many times, and he even pulled a gun on her and his children when she was in their home. She had been beaten and abused and always felt her life was in peril. This was the treacherous path the pain of divorce had landed her on, but today she is safe and no longer in that relationship. She now spends every day praising and thanking Jesus for capturing her heart and holding her in His arms, redirecting her path, and writing a better ending to her story.

> Forgive yourself and accept God's forgiveness today.

I too had to make a lot of hard decisions to turn things around, and I am still in the process of mending some of the problems I created by letting my guard down on what I knew was right. I'm still far from perfect and even still involved in some things I know I should probably change in my life. But I also know that as I continue to lean into God, put my faith in Him, serve in ministry, follow God's call on my life to write and speak His hope into hurting hearts, as well as surround myself with people and things that will fuel my faith instead of put out my fire, God will do a mighty work in me and my life—irrespective of me, my choices, or my imperfections. I can already see the good things He is weaving to help me reshape myself and my future one day at a time. My heart has been in turmoil, but God has been pulling me closer and closer, convicting my spirit with clarity and direction and helping me find the courage and strength to see each day as a chance to begin anew.

I'm so thankful for the reminder that God's love never fails and we get to start fresh every new day. In Lamentations, Jeremiah was in anguish, grieving and lamenting the fall of Jerusalem to Babylon. But something changed inside him, and he said, "Yet I still dare to hope when I remember this: The faithful love of the LORD never ends! His mercies never cease. Great is his faithfulness; his mercies begin afresh each morning" (3:21–23). He paused in the midst of his grief and despair and remembered he could still find hope regardless of his circumstances and emotions. Even in the worst of times, God is always faithful.

Every single day God's mercies are new for me and for you. We can never mess up enough to void this scriptural promise. His mercy and compassion are endless. He wants us to make good choices and avoid patterns of sin, but His love is still unconditional.

You Are Dearly Loved

No matter where you are right now, how you're feeling, what coping mechanisms you've turned to, or the number of mistakes you've made, never forget you are loved by the One who gave His life for yours. Victory over our emotions, desires, sins, choices, and temptations may come slowly, but it will come. I have certainly not landed in a place in which I've overcome the past and never worry, doubt myself, wither with lack of confidence, make mistakes, or juggle regrets. All my problems aren't solved, and life is still difficult in many ways. But God is with each of us every step of the way, and we can count on the truth that our heavenly Father's love, grace, and compassion will never change. We can have hope for the present and the future because of Him.

Never think you are the only one who has sinned out of the depths of your pain because, sweet sister, you are not. And it's okay. You are okay. Life will be okay. You are a good person, and life will be good again. Forgive yourself and accept God's forgiveness today.

Major trauma in any form will affect us all in different ways, push us in directions we never deemed possible, hinder good decision-making, riddle us with battle scars, and maybe slowly turn us into someone we don't even recognize or like. Being Christian does not shield us from the pain of divorce or the temptations that lead to poor choices or damaging behaviors, but our foundational beliefs can bring us back to putting on the armor of God. Our faith can compel us to keep pushing through the battle and becoming the person we want to be.

The passage about putting on the armor of God—the belt of truth, body armor of righteousness, shoes of peace, shield of faith, helmet of salvation, and sword of the Spirit—is a popular piece of Scripture. The instruction it holds is unsurpassed and can be the determining factor for how we progress through this journey of divorce. Out of sheer devastation, hopelessness, and confusion, I pulled away from some of this armor rather than putting it on daily. But I and others—possibly even you—have learned the hard way that this is not the best thing to do. We can't stand firm in the wake of divorce if we put down the armor God has given us for the battle.

I love the way *The Message* expresses this passage.

A Fight to the Finish

And that about wraps it up. God is strong, and he wants you strong. So take everything the Master has set out for you, well-made weapons of the best materials. And put them to use so you will be able to stand up to everything the Devil throws your way. This is no afternoon athletic contest that we'll walk away from and forget about in a couple of hours. This is for keeps, a life-or-death fight to the finish against the Devil and all his angels.

Be prepared. You're up against far more than you can handle on your own. Take all the help you can get, every weapon God has issued, so that when it's all over but the shouting you'll still be on your feet. Truth, righteousness, peace, faith, and salvation are more than words. Learn how to apply them. You'll need them throughout your life. God's Word is an *indispensable* weapon. In the same way, prayer is essential in this ongoing warfare. Pray hard and long. Pray for your brothers and sisters. Keep your eyes open. Keep each other's spirits up so that no one falls behind or drops out. (Eph. 6:10–18)

We are at war, although not with spouses, court systems, mortgage companies, or in-laws, which may feel like our flesh-and-blood enemies. We are at war with the "evil rulers and authorities of the unseen world, against mighty powers in this dark world, and against evil spirits in the heavenly places" (v. 12). We are at war with an enemy who wants us to continue feeling discouraged, hopeless, helpless, sad, and alone. An enemy who wants us to feel so guilty that we close ourselves off from our faith and others and assume the worst of God instead of the best. An enemy who wants us to turn our backs on God and put down our armor.

Put on your armor, and be ready for anything the devil throws at you. Be prepared because the battle is hard and we can't fight it alone. Yet we can all shout victory one day.

> He is never too far away to hear our cries for rescue, and we are never too far from His grace to be forgiven.

Your "enemies" may be different from mine or someone else's, but we are all fighting one enemy who has the same fate planned for all of us. He would have us live apart from God in sadness and sorrow, weighted down by the past, the present, and the fear of the future, with no peace, hope, or happiness in our hearts.

But take heart! We are not left to that fate. Wearing the armor of God, we can stand firm. Stand strong. Overcome. Be confident. And build new lives not without problems but with hearts full of happiness, joy, and contentment.

Ephesians 6:18 says, "Pray in the Spirit on all occasions with all kinds of prayers and requests. With this in mind, be alert and always keep on praying for all the Lord's people" (NIV). The same verse in *The Message* reads, "In the same way, prayer is essential in this ongoing warfare. Pray hard and long. Pray for your brothers and sisters. Keep your eyes open. Keep each other's spirits up so that no one falls behind or drops out."

It's never too late to turn things around or for God to rescue you from shame and guilt and all the other emotions stealing your joy. You may have made mistakes, but you are not a mistake, and our mistakes do not define us. No matter how far we have fallen or how deep in the pit we are, we are never too far away to call out to God and see those rays of hope. He is never too far away to hear our cries for rescue, and we are never too far from His grace to be forgiven. When we seek Him, He will answer in love.

The best time to cry out to God is when our hearts are broken because they are already cracked wide open to receive His love and mercy. Psalm 50:15 says, "Call on me when you are in trouble, and I will rescue you, and you will give me glory." God already knows our troubles and our needs, but miracles happen when we recognize how much we need Him and let Him know.

No matter where you find yourself today, stop and pray. Pray daily. Pray hourly if need be. Pray hard and long. In fact, just pray without ceasing and simply never say "Amen."

Happiness Prompters

- Start a new exercise program today, and don't allow yourself to make excuses. Exercise has a profound effect

on our happiness and well-being and has even proved to be an effective method for helping overcome depression because it releases endorphins that make us feel happier.[3]

- Write a personal declaration statement, which is simply a letter to yourself that defines where you've been, who you are, and who you want to be. This will be a tool you can use daily to help you replace all the lies about who you think you are or how life will be and help you start putting the past behind you. It is also an effective way to help you replace an old belief system with a new one and equip you to continue to stay hopeful and positive even in the midst of life's upsets.

- Pray for God's peace, forgiveness, and comfort to fill your heart as you get started on this task. Begin your declaration with acknowledging any mistakes, regrets, or lies about yourself or your future while remembering your declaration is between you and God alone. Then start making a list of all the good things about yourself that you know to be true but often forget, such as *"I am a good person. I am a loving mother. I am perfectly made in God's image. I have unique talents. I am good with my finances. I am great at my job. I am a good boss. I am a talented cook. I always treat others with love and kindness. I have a servant's heart. I will not allow lies or hurt from past experiences steal my joy today. I will survive this situation and will thrive and be happy!* Then in paragraph form, elaborate on each positive trait. Write as if you were giving yourself a pep talk. Then put your per-sonal declaration where you can always see it—on your fridge or on a pretty printable graphic in a frame—and repeat your declaration out loud every day. This is you declaring you are in control of your life and it is going to be great!

Healing Steps

1. What do you feel most guilty about? Although the reasons for our guilt are usually something we'd like to push under the carpet and forget, dealing with them is the only way to overcome guilt's toll on our hearts. Be honest with yourself and God in prayer and ask for His forgiveness and grace; then accept them once and for all. Also consider looking up Scripture verses that remind you of how God loves and values you unconditionally.

2. How does hearing the stories of other women help you feel less guilty, recognizing everyone makes mistakes? Reflect on which story gave you the most hope about overcoming shame and guilt and how you can apply the tips shared to your life.

3. How do you talk to yourself? Are you harsh and critical or compassionate and forgiving? Commit to being aware of self-condemning thoughts, and transform them each time into something positive about yourself instead.

Caring for You

Read Ephesians 6:10–18 again, in several translations if desired. Picture yourself standing tall and putting on the armor of God in the ways this passage instructs us to. Each morning when you get dressed, mentally dress yourself in this armor while you are putting on your clothes. Ask God to help you fight whatever battles the day brings. Pray long and pray hard.

Chapter 8

Girl, You Are Not Crazy

With great trauma comes great stress. These two things combined can sometimes make us feel like we're losing our minds altogether. We can't process emotions. We can't get over the trauma. We can't figure out how to feel or act. We can't stop crying. We can't understand why our spouse did what he did or why he is hurting us the way he is. We can barely get ourselves out of bed in the morning—or evening. We can't keep all the details of life straight, which we now have to manage. We forget everything. We feel ill-quipped to make decisions. We can't fix all the problems in our lives no matter how hard we try. We can't figure out why we feel the way we do or why we can't get along with a former spouse—or why we want him back after how much he has devastated us. We can't fix or change other people.

We can't make our spouse love us or want us no matter what we do. We don't feel equipped to be a single mom or single woman, and we worry about our children's hearts. We feel painfully alone and simply want to feel better, even if only for one day or one hour. We can't let go of the dreams we had for the future. If we've been married to a narcissist, we can't figure out which way is up, what is true or false, how to stop being mentally and emotionally manipulated and gaslighted, or how to navigate the journey when every conversation leaves us feeling confused. Life seems to be attacking us from every direction. It's enough to make even the sanest person feel insane.

Trying to handle so much at once, without the power to make anything different, can be maddening and lead to serious self-doubt. *Crazy* might sum up how we feel about ourselves, so read these next sentences closely. In fact, read them several times if you need to.

You are not crazy. You are not crazy for feeling crazy. And most of all, you are not alone in those feelings of craziness. You've gone through something traumatic, and it takes a toll.

PTSD Is for Real

The end of any relationship can be traumatic, but divorce typically packs the hardest punch to our mental and emotional states.

Divorce will be experienced differently by everyone, especially depending on how the marriage was before it ended, the treatment a spouse received, or the reason the marriage ended. For example, maybe your marriage was loving but then suddenly the love stopped, or maybe an affair took place and lies and deceit ran rampant. Maybe your spouse was a narcissist and emotionally and mentally manipulated you for years, or maybe your spouse was physically abusive or struggled with addictions. Maybe your spouse left a note saying he didn't want to be married anymore and simply walked away. Regardless of the circumstances, toxic trauma can settle deep in our souls, and we start living in a state of confusion and hurt.

As the first year of my separation dragged by torturously, I lived in a continuous state of bewilderment and disorientation, hoping for the best but deep down always expecting the worst. I lost fifteen pounds because I couldn't eat due to stress, and as I shared earlier, I suffered from insomnia and depression. I couldn't get control of my emotions no matter how hard I tried. I felt as if I were caught up in a hurricane, spinning out of control and having no idea how to rise above it, never able to catch my breath. I never knew what to believe or how to deal with each new piece of debris that was flung into my path.

Over the next couple of years, drawn-out legal battles ensued out of desperation for financial support, adding fuel to the flames of rejection, fear, insecurity, sadness, and worthlessness burning in my heart. Back and forth to court and lawyers' offices for years, until the day I found out it had all been pointless for several reasons beyond my control and loopholes in the legal system. That discovery sent me off the deep end and into sheer despondency. My level of trauma, frustration, sadness, shock, anger, and grief hit an all-time high. I lost it. A full-blown panic attack hit hard. I couldn't take any more.

Although I wasn't physically on a battlefield, I felt my life was in danger. My physical and emotional well-being were in danger as well as my children's. I could see constant threats looming in the distance—countless threats to our livelihood and the probability of more pain. The psychological blows were unceasing, and although the wounds were invisible, the pain and scars were real. My heart and mind reached levels of fatigue I didn't know were possible, and on some days I felt physically ill, exhausted, and a little bit crazy.

Within the past year, I finally became aware of the fact I had been suffering from a form of PTSD (post-traumatic stress disorder). I wasn't officially diagnosed by a doctor, yet after much research of the symptoms and after conversations with my counselor that unearthed a lot of eye-opening distinctions, I am confident this has become part of my story.

Although I've always tried to be strong and keep pushing through each problem, a lot of psychological and emotional damage left gaping injuries on my heart and mind. I have become acutely aware of how I react when a trigger sets off my emotions and when memories transport me to a bad place mentally. I have implemented a practice to immediately pray for God to continue to help me overcome these stumbling blocks. These things are hard to admit because I'd rather say I was strong and unshakable and cruised through this storm on faith alone. But that would be far from true. Divorce swings in like a wrecking ball, and nothing in our lives can escape the impact of its destruction, no matter how hard we try to keep up the strong facade.

However, rather than being ashamed about it, I let this discovery help me remember to give more grace to myself when my emotions get the better of me, when my fears start consuming my thoughts, when I feel guilty for mistakes I make. This realization opened the door for me to see and understand myself a little better, begin to heal, and truly believe I wasn't going crazy after all.

Post-traumatic stress disorder, although most-often mentioned when referring to military veterans, can be a real experience of anyone who has been through something traumatic. The end of a marriage definitely falls into the traumatic experience category, especially if it happened abruptly or when infidelity, dishonesty, narcissism, abandonment, pornography, or substance abuse occurred and/or if major legal proceedings and court decisions regarding finances or children were involved.

Post-traumatic stress is a normal emotional and psychological reaction to any traumatic, painful, or shocking experience that exists outside someone's normal life experiences. People who experience a traumatic event will often react with shock, anger, nervousness, fear, and guilt, similar in some ways to the five stages of grief.[1] According to the National Institute of Mental Health, most people with these reactions will recover in time, but for people with PTSD, these feelings can cause them to have difficulty living normal lives.[2] PTSD occurs when the mind simply cannot process the trauma it has experienced.

Healing is a process, not a destination.

In my case, I could barely function at all during my first year of separation, much less process all that happened, but I did get better over time. So many women have told me they felt the same way. Barely able to get out of bed in the morning, even months after the spouse left, unable to face the reality of what was happening, let alone grasp how to manage life going forward. Incapable of going one day, sometimes even one hour, without bursting into tears, then feeling like a frustrated fool for not being able to keep it together. Feeling like they were living in a foggy haze, incapable of thinking clearly or being happy, and often making unfortunate decisions to cope.

Countless women struggle with undiagnosed PTSD, and some fall into a pattern of bad decision-making after going through the trauma of divorce, depending on the severity of the situation, as I mentioned in the previous chapter. A close look at your symptoms can indicate PTSD; however, a doctor's visit is always best to not only diagnose PTSD but also help you determine the best treatment and healing plan for you. Symptoms of PTSD after divorce may include overly negative thoughts about oneself or the world, exaggerated blaming of self or others, isolation, irritability or aggression, paranoia, risky or destructive behavior, difficulty concentrating, and insomnia.[3] High anxiety levels and stress are usually present, and even chronic pain can occur.

According to psychotherapist Toni Coleman, "If a person goes through an acrimonious, drawn-out, expensive, time-consuming, and lifestyle-altering divorce … it can lead to debilitating symptoms of anxiety in which PTSD takes root. These symptoms are the result of the divorce trauma being embedded in the person's subconscious mind and then experienced as recurrent fears and bad memories."[4] For obvious reasons, this can make it difficult for a person to move on. Even worse, it can affect your health, which is something we often don't realize.

Dr. James S. Gordon, author of *The Transformation: Discovering Wholeness and Healing after Trauma* and founder of the Center for Mind-Body Medicine, spoke about the effects of trauma on our bodies: "It's true that some experiences are most obviously traumatic, like rape or war, but things like dealing with a serious illness in yourself or a family member, the death of someone close, the breakup of a significant relationship, or even losing a job or leaving a community that's very important to you can be traumatic." He also found that the negative psychological and physical effects of any type of trauma may not go away on their own and can extend far beyond the period of time when the trauma actually happened, which can result in PTSD.

Dr. Gordon also concluded that any type of trauma affects our minds and our bodies. He says, "Everything that happens to us emotionally or psychologically happens to our bodies as well. It's all connected. If you look at people who go into a fight, flight, or freeze response, just look at the way they hold their bodies—they're tense, they're tight, their whole body is set up to protect them from a predator. And I believe this tension is connected with the traumatic experience in ways we don't completely understand."[5]

Dr. Shaili Jain, associate professor at Stanford School of Medicine, PTSD specialist and trauma scientist, and author of *The Unspeakable Mind*, found that when "traumatic thoughts and memories remain unspeakable or unthinkable for too long, they often impede our brain's natural process of recovery after trauma. They become stuck points that inhibit the mental reintegration that is needed for healing to occur." She followed up by saying that PTSD "brings disruption to hormone secretion, neurochemistry, and immune system functioning, all of which contribute to diseased cells, organs, and other bodily systems.... Up to 35% of chronic pain patients also have PTSD, and there is an even higher overlap between fibromyalgia and PTSD."[6]

PTSD is more common than you might think. My friend Natalie was diagnosed with PTSD after her divorce. Although she came to understand her emotions more, she still struggles occasionally. When she feels even the slightest hint of dishonesty or manipulation, her PTSD is triggered, and her emotions go from zero to sixty in a heartbeat. She sometimes reacts out of proportion to the circumstance and later regrets her actions.

Although she hasn't overcome this tendency, the good news is she has recognized it, as I have in myself. She realizes she easily reacts to triggers, which bring back all the painful memories of what she went through and cause her to think, feel, and act irrationally. She has learned that when that happens, she should apologize to the person she was dealing with. Her goal is to live acutely aware of this tendency so she can address it before she overreacts, instead of after.

Heather struggled with PTSD symptoms as well, and insomnia plagued her. In an attempt to cope, she isolated herself from her friends and family and avoided situations that triggered certain reactions. She began dealing with anxiety attacks for the first time, to the point where she couldn't think, hear, or see certain things. She chose to begin seeing a therapist and is working hard toward recovery and healing.

The abusive situation Patti had to endure was heartbreaking. Her husband still lived in their home for months after telling her he wanted out of the marriage. He lived out a pattern of being verbally and physically abusive to her and her children. She tried to protect the children as much as she could while living in a nightmare that seemed to have no end. She put locks on their bedroom doors, but he would break in, causing her to live in a state of fear. She eventually went to a Christian counselor, who prescribed two medications to help her control her emotions. But although those things had some benefits, the only thing that truly helped her was focusing on Jesus and her faith. Gradually she found the courage to get a court order to get her husband out of the house and change the locks and garage codes shortly after. Even though all this happened almost three years ago, Patti's body still has similar reactions when she has to interact with him or when something triggers a painful memory or fear.

Cyndi was diagnosed with PTSD due to her husband's infidelity. Every time something triggered her memories of what happened, she would start hyperventilating and have an anxiety attack. Her counselor gave her tips for reducing anxiety and encouraged her to be mindful of what was around her instead of letting her fears get the better of her. The counselor suggested she concentrate on all five senses and ask herself questions like *What do I hear right now?* and *What do I see?* Since Cyndi loved relaxing in a hot bath, her counselor inspired her to treat herself more often. Each time, she would light a candle to see and smell, fill the tub with lots of bubbles to feel, listen to soft music, and enjoy a peppermint candy for taste. Again, focusing on her senses. Then she tries to think about all her blessings and tells herself everything is okay in that moment, which helps her calm her anxiety. She reminds herself that although life might seem out of control, she can narrow her focus to what is in front of her and notice how God is taking care of her.

> Either we can let divorce destroy us,
> or we can let it make us stronger.

Carla was diagnosed with PTSD and continually works on processing her emotions. But she admitted she doesn't talk about her diagnosis much because PTSD "is an invisible issue, frequently misunderstood and stigmatized." We feel like we should be strong and able to handle life better. We get embarrassed about our over-reactions to situations that dig up old feelings, fears, and insecurities. We may feel ashamed when something bad happens and we can't cry. We fear what other people will think if we tell them we are struggling with this "mental disorder," which only exacerbates our insecurity and loneliness. It's likely that many women, myself included, think we need to keep our PTSD a secret.

One friend shared that she didn't believe her ex-husband was a narcissist but she could definitely relate to having symptoms of PTSD. Each time he would text or call her, her hands and feet would become cold instantly and her heart would race as she feared what he was going to say or do to her next. All the trauma she had endured from her husband's emotional abuse, betrayal, and abandonment laid the foundation for even the smallest thing to trigger her most painful memories and feelings.

After I recognized I was experiencing PTSD, it was so helpful to finally realize I am a trigger queen. Owning it.

If I suspect someone is being dishonest with me, I assume that person is lying about everything under the sun. I have a serious problem trusting anyone, sometimes even my closest friends. If I don't get an invite to a social outing or I am even inadvertently left out of a group text, my insecurities spike. I begin thinking I'm replaceable and that my absence in someone's life or my friend group wouldn't be noticed. I immediately feel like I might as well eat a worm and die because surely I have no friends whatsoever and I'm going to end up alone one day with fourteen cats in a one-room house. I've even accused beloved family members of being somewhat dishonest about a situation when in reality they were not. If my children disagree with something I've said or done, my mind erupts, convincing me I'm a terrible mother and my children are going to leave me too, which clearly is ridiculous. I could keep listing examples of my thoughts going to crazy places because of the emotional trauma I've experienced, but I'll stop there. Let's just say … girl, it's a problem.

Fortunately, like many of the women who have shared their stories in this book, I finally concluded that certain situations— even minor ones—hold the potential to bring back every emotion, insecurity, and fear I thought I had dealt with and overcome. My heart has been so damaged that even the smallest trigger can send me in a direction I don't want to go. I've had to come to grips with the fact that everyone else is not always the problem—sometimes the problem is with me and my tattered heart. My faith, friends, and family became my lifeline, and I held onto them as tightly as I could since I knew they would love me despite my PTSD reactions.

Healing is a process, not a destination. Recovering from the trauma of abuse, separation, abandonment, and divorce is hard. Recovering from being married to a narcissist, abuser, serial adulterer, or a neglectful, unloving husband can seem impossible. Recovering from the life-altering symptoms of PTSD can seem beyond hope. We may wonder if we can ever feel normal and open our hearts to fully loving and trusting anyone ever again. Fortunately for most people, the fears and triggered emotions after traumatic events will subside, but for some who develop PTSD, the intense emotions and disturbing thoughts can hang on even years after the end of the marriage. But the good news is that nothing is impossible with God! We can all recover in our own time with perseverance and a commitment to leaning into our faith.

PTSD is not a fun subject to talk about! But it is an important one. Yet on a more positive note, I discovered something awesome!

Upon researching post-divorce PTSD online, I came across something that made my heart leap. Two words radically changed my perspective: *post-traumatic growth*.

Growth? Growth, after abandonment? Growth, after having my heart shattered? Growth, after finding myself alone, hurt, and betrayed, especially in midlife and during menopause? Growth, after having my family torn apart? Growth, after practically drowning in the cesspools of fear, insecurity, and sorrow? Growth, after nearly losing everything I owned? Growth, after divorce? Yes! Yes! Yes! Yes! Yes! Yes! And yes! And it can happen for you too!

Experiencing Growth after Trauma

Post-traumatic growth (PTG) is the opposite of post-traumatic stress. Where PTSD becomes an obstacle to living happy lives, post-traumatic growth helps us blossom and thrive, building even more meaningful lives than we had before. According to Karen Covy, a divorce adviser, attorney, and coach, "Instead of being crushed by tragedy, people who experience post traumatic growth transcend tragedy."[7]

Neuroscience research has proved that trauma causes dark tar-like masses to form in the brain. In a sense they act like glue and keep the brain stuck in a state of trauma. This can make decision-making difficult and can even cause the brain to keep reliving the trauma. However, research shows that if we remove or deal with the associated emotions, the brain can dissolve the trauma mass by releasing hormones.[8] "People tend to have the most difficulty healing from trauma deliberately caused by others,"[9] whether physical, emotional, or verbal, and especially by someone they once loved and trusted.

But as we deal with our emotions, transform our patterns of thinking, and take control of what we can, post-traumatic growth can begin to sprout.

Betrayal, infidelity, dishonesty, abuse, neglect, and abandonment are all wounds that cause deep trauma. Yet they are wounds we can heal from *and* grow from, no matter how deeply they've penetrated our hearts.

When we find ourselves at a crossroads in life, we each have a life-altering decision to make. Either we can let divorce destroy us, or we can let it make us stronger. Either we can let someone steal our self-worth and determine our future happiness, or we can let our value be found in Christ alone and trust He has an amazing plan for our new lives. Either we can retreat, or we can advance into meaningful lives and embrace every opportunity for happiness. We can either let divorce make us bitter or let it make us better. There is always purpose in our pain, but we have to choose to look for it and believe that it helps us avoid letting bitterness take root.

Wikipedia describes post-traumatic growth as "positive psychological change experienced as a result of adversity and other challenges in order to rise to a higher level of functioning.... Posttraumatic growth involves 'life-changing' psychological shifts in thinking and relating to the world, that contribute to a personal process of change, that is deeply meaningful."[10]

There was nothing I wanted more than to grow from my experience rather than letting it take me down. I wanted to not only survive the experience but also thrive on the other side of it. Don't you? If you want that badly enough and you are willing to put in the hard work, it can happen for you. However, you have to set yourself up for growth, and there are a few factors that affect our ability to deal with trauma—the most important one being mind-set.

As I've mentioned many times so far, our thoughts have power. Thoughts are like wheels taking us in one direction or another. They can lead us into temptation, negativity, grief, and disappointment. Or they can lead us into yearning after God, thinking optimistically, and living joy-filled, positive lives regardless of our circumstances.

A positive mind-set is the root of starting over well after divorce. No matter how terrible our marriage, separation, and/or divorce may have been or how much hurt we've endured, we can all grow personally, spiritually, and emotionally. We can choose to rebuild our lives if we view our situation as not just the end of a marriage but the beginning of our new lives.

You Can Grow and Thrive

Post-traumatic growth is a process. It takes an ongoing determination to be resilient, and when the grief process subsides, it requires the determination to bounce back and move forward with optimism. A positive mind-set is empowering because believing it is possible to grow and thrive after divorce is crucial to our success.

PTG has also been called "benefit finding," and according to various psychology studies, these benefits generally fit into five categories:

- **Feeling stronger and more confident and tapping into our hidden abilities and strengths.** For example, we realize if we can survive divorce, one of the most painful and traumatic experiences someone can go through, then we can survive anything.

- **Greater appreciation for life.** Once we've experienced great loss, we treasure the things that are important to us even more.
- **Strengthening positive relationships.** For example, we find our true friends, who will stick with us through thick and thin. We become more compassionate and empathetic.
- **Learning to live for the moment and getting our priorities straight.** This includes putting ourselves and the important people in our lives at the top of the list. We gain a better perspective on life and what's important.
- **Growing spiritually.** The demise of a marriage is traumatizing and can land us in the deepest pit of discouragement and hopelessness we've ever experienced. The journey to get out of the pit is hard and long, and at some point we realize we can't do it alone.[11]

As of the writing of this book, it's been four and a half years since my husband left. On one hand, it feels like I've been on this broken path much longer, but on the other hand, I feel like it just started yesterday. I am able to envision and feel every detail of the day he walked out of our kitchen for the last time. But I have absolutely benefited in all the ways mentioned above, and for that I am incredibly thankful. But maybe as you read that list, you shook your head and thought, *That's great for you, Tracie, but very unlikely to happen*

*for me. I can't imagine feeling confident again, appreciating life, having
great relationships, having a positive perspective, or growing spiritually.
Not gonna happen.*

I understand.

I had the same thoughts a few years ago. Yet over time I saw
other women growing and thriving and enjoying life even after the
worst of divorce experiences. That awareness, coupled with God's
promise in Jeremiah 29:11 that He had an amazing future planned
for me, helped me wrap one tiny pinky finger around the notion that
maybe, just maybe, I could survive, grow, and thrive as His plans fell
into place for my life. This promise is not meant only for me and
other lucky women, but it is for you too!

You can do this! Start with small steps toward rebuilding your
confidence. Call a friend once a day to encourage her, because blessing others always blesses us in return. Master a new skill. Start seeing
a counselor. Join that in-person support group and build camarade-
rie. Intentionally focus on all the blessings in your life. Be cognizant
of your thinking patterns. Notice if they are positive or negative, and
if they're negative, start trying to transform those thoughts. Spend
time in God's Word and with other believers, pray often, and attend
church.

Every healing journey has to begin somewhere, and even the
tiniest step is one step forward. Even if all you can do right now
is wrap your pinky finger around a shred of hope as I did, do it.
Memorize Jeremiah 29:11: "I know what I'm doing. I have it all
planned out—plans to take care of you, not abandon you, plans to
give you the future you hope for" (THE MESSAGE). Recite it daily,
especially on the worst of days, and believe it with all your heart.

Today I feel stronger and more confident. I have so much appreciation for life and all the people in it. I have developed a stronger passion and compassion for people in general but especially for women walking this hard road. I have become less judgmental and more open minded and accepting. I live for the moment and try to keep a positive outlook, even in the face of new adversities. Although it's often a challenge to remember that God is good when life isn't, I try to remind myself that even during those seasons when I was not making my faith a priority, He never left me, which motivates me to continue leaning into my faith.

> Girl, you are not crazy, and you are not incapable of moving forward and living a happy, joy-filled life.

I wouldn't be where I am today without Jesus. I could not have walked this journey in my own strength, courage, and capabilities. It's not easy to push through and come out stronger, happier, and more content, but it is possible! I didn't do everything right, and I don't have a magic formula, but through faith, perseverance, and a burning desire to be resilient, we can all grow with the goal of loving God, loving ourselves, and loving life again.

Will you allow yourself to trust God has a beautiful future in store for you, even though your worst fears may have come true? Will you have faith that you are not an exception to the rule—that you will overcome and thrive through the love and support of Christ, family, and friends? Will you love yourself as God loves you? Will you put your hope in the only One who gives hope? If your answer is yes to these questions, you just made progress. Smiles.

Divorce is a traumatic event. Never let anyone convince you otherwise. If you've questioned what is wrong with you when you feel depressed or experience physical pain or discomfort, the best thing you can do is care enough about yourself to acknowledge and accept you've experienced great trauma and realize the need to take care of you. You deserve to make yourself a priority. Don't be ashamed to go to the doctor and be honest about what you are experiencing. It could be the best thing you do for yourself, your future, and even your children.

Girl, you are not crazy, and you are not incapable of moving forward and living a happy, joy-filled life. You *will* heal and recover and love your life again if that is your goal and you strive for it! New hope and life can cause the scars of divorce to fade over time and open the door for post-traumatic growth to be a part of your story.

Happiness Prompters

- Make a list of the textures, scents, sounds, views, and places that bring you joy. Figure out a way to enjoy them regularly.
- This might sound strange, but make a mental inventory of the bad things you've experienced. Yet rather than

focusing on the bad memory, think about how much you've accomplished since then and how many significant challenges you've already overcome. Be proud of yourself. You are a champion. Let these thoughts give you courage to keep taking life one day at a time and believing in yourself.

Healing Steps

1. Whether you have been clinically diagnosed with PTSD or not, are there certain symptoms, behaviors, or thoughts you struggle with that could be related to it? Over the next few days and weeks, try to be aware of any PTSD symptoms you may be experiencing or if certain triggers set off your emotions or behaviors. Ask God to help you redirect your thoughts and emotions in a constructive way each time something happens.

2. What positive coping methods have you tried? How have they helped in your healing process? Write down three goals for yourself for how to turn these methods into habits to help keep you on the road to recovery.

3. How do you feel learning that post-traumatic growth is a real thing? Hopefully it gives you great hope! Look back at what this chapter says about the benefits derived from PTG, and write out five declarations for yourself. Commit to striving toward these growth results. Anytime you start doubting you will survive and grow, revisit your declarations for reassurance.

Caring for You

Be a blessing to yourself today. Treat yourself to a special dessert, take a long walk in the woods or by the water, soak in a bubble bath, buy yourself something new, or get your nails manicured. You deserve it.

Chapter 9

Love Conquers All

Love is not always a warm, fuzzy word, especially when we're feeling unloved by the ones we loved most. In fact, reading that word right now might prompt some serious eye-rolling because our thoughts generally turn to romantic love, which likely is missing from your life right now. But love is the one thing that will carry us through this journey well and help us manage all those doubts, insecurities, and fears. And that love comes in many forms.

One of the most heart-wrenching concerns single moms have is how divorce is going to affect their children and their ability to be good mothers. We long to ease the suffering of our children, but our minds are in a battle, often telling us we aren't doing enough.

I certainly struggled with this, and if you're a mother, I imagine you have too. Our children were twenty-two, twenty, and sixteen when my husband left, and they were devastated. Their pain was excruciating to watch, and they each handled it in different ways. Since they were older, I couldn't simply tell them Mommy and Daddy decided to part ways all of a sudden. I couldn't make up excuses for their father leaving. I couldn't hide the lies or my devastation any longer. I had to be honest. And it was hard.

Sharing the painful details of what caused our separation was horrible. Hearing them was probably even worse. I had secretly struggled for years, hiding what was going on behind closed doors to keep anyone else from hurting. Admittedly, part of me felt a secret sense of relief that it was over, but it was shocking news to my children. Their father's departure left them feeling confused, broken, sad, and insecure. Victims of circumstances they did nothing to cause.

Every child regardless of age will face unique challenges when a family falls apart. And as much as we may want to be perfect mothers, it is an impossible feat. If we hold ourselves to unattainable standards, we set ourselves up for defeat.

So what do we do? How do we avoid feeling like we are failing? How do we handle the situation in an age-appropriate way? And how do we not drive ourselves crazy with self-doubt and obsessive worry over being a good parent? How do we get beyond desperately wishing the situation were different for the children's sake, if for no other reason?

The most important thing we can do to get our children through this type of trauma with as few scars as possible can be summed up in one word.

Love.

Love your children. Love yourself. Love your God.

Love Your Children

Loving our children through divorce is the most precious gift we can give them. Love becomes their coping mechanism whether they are two years old or forty-two. Loving them not only means making them a priority but also making their feelings a priority.

As I waded through the rocky waters of separation, I can't say I always loved perfectly. I'm sure I talked to my daughters and my son a little too much and shared too many details because I desperately needed someone to talk to and I wanted them to understand the pain we were experiencing. I needed to process feelings and thoughts with someone. I couldn't afford a counselor, and my kids were so sweet to always listen and offer encouragement, love, support, and empathy. My prayer is that we all helped one another through it, but I'm sure the weight of my pain and sorrow was heavy for them. In fact, one day when I was yet again unable to stop crying over the most recent hurtful event, one of my daughters gently interrupted my self-pity tantrum and reminded me that I was not the only one going through this terrible experience. Ouch.

> Loving our children through divorce is the most precious gift we can give them.

That's difficult to divulge, because I had put my children's feelings and needs first for more than two decades. I had always poured myself into being the most loving and attentive mom I could be, and now I had gotten so caught up in my own trauma that I was not being as attentive to theirs as I should have been. From that day forward, I made every effort to put their feelings ahead of my own, say only what needed to be shared, and stay acutely aware of their emotional needs. I couldn't simply assume they were doing okay because I didn't see evidence that they weren't.

Nothing mattered more to me than my children's happiness and helping them get through this horrific situation. But tragedy can blind us to how other people feel because we get so consumed with our own pain. It's like being hit by a Mack truck but then being expected to get up and tend to the injuries of others instead of our own. It's certainly not easy to pull ourselves out of our own heads and remember to place our focus on loving and caring for the hearts of those in our lives. However, when it comes to our children's emotional well-being, no matter what age they are, it is so necessary.

If you don't have children, your heart may break for how your situation is affecting your family and friends because a divorce affects everyone in our lives in different ways and we don't want anyone we love to be in pain. If you do have children, though, I assume you have shouldered the same emotional burdens for them as I did. A mother's love is immeasurable and infinite. When her children hurt, the pain in her own heart is magnified, especially when she feels helpless to mend their deepest invisible wounds. Children can carry the weight of everyone's grief, and knowing this can be the heaviest burden on a mama's heart. No matter how much we do or how perfectly we try to handle the situation and our children's emotions, we may never feel we're doing well enough.

Every time one of our kids acts out, rebels, shuts down, or makes a bad decision, we blame the divorce and maybe ourselves. We wonder whether they're permanently scarred, and we shoulder part of the blame. We face an internal struggle about whether we're being too lenient or too strict. We are edgy and emotionally unstable, sometimes snapping at them and then feeling guilty and incapable of loving as we should. We beat ourselves up. We collapse at the end of the day in despair, worrying about how well we handled the challenges of the day and the demands of parenting. We look ourselves in the mirror and blurt out, "What is wrong with you?!"

We may even ask God why in the world He made us a mother to these precious children when we're clearly not qualified or capable—especially under these circumstances. We question our ability to co-parent successfully, struggle with being away from the children on a regular basis—especially on holidays—and fret over knowing they are possibly with the new woman in our ex-husband's life. We may say too much or make negative comments about their dad and later regret what we said, wondering how our words are affecting them. We can worry ourselves to death if we're not careful, so it's important to remember this is just a hard season and it too shall pass.

In Ecclesiastes 3:1 we read, "For everything there is a season, a time for every activity under heaven." The rest of this popular passage goes on to say there is a time to be born and a time to die, to plant and harvest, to tear down and build up, to cry and laugh, and so on (see vv. 2–8). This passage reminds us that God has arranged every detail of our lives and that everything happens according to His will and in His timing.

And guess what? Your divorce is not a shock to God.

> *Divorce does not diminish your value as a woman or a mom.*

This is a hard fact to hear, much less accept. It causes us to get all twisted up inside and question God's ways and maybe even His love for us. It messes with our minds as we try to make sense of the questions intruding on our thoughts. *Why would God let me marry this man if He knew this would happen? Why would He let me experience such pain? Why didn't He protect me and guide my decisions?* And if a second marriage didn't work out, we might wonder, *Why did He let that happen to me again?*

God doesn't want divorce for any of His children, but the fact is we live in a broken world and we all have free will to make our own choices. Things happen in this world that aren't fair, and God's heart breaks when ours are broken. We find proof of this in Isaiah 63:8–9: "He became their Savior. In all their troubles, he was troubled, too. He didn't send someone else to help them. He did it himself, in person. Out of his own love and pity he redeemed them. He rescued them and carried them along for a long, long time" (THE MESSAGE). No matter what happens and regardless of the underlying reasons for a relationship breakdown or who was most at fault, God never stops loving us. He always offers compassion, not condemnation. He cares about our broken hearts and our deepest worries, and that alone is comforting to remember.

Divorce does not diminish your value as a woman or a mom. Just because your marriage didn't work doesn't mean you are now ill-equipped to love your children and be the mom God knew you could be. It doesn't mean you did the wrong thing. Sometimes relationships don't work out, people change, and bad things happen to good people. **Divorce doesn't label us as broken. It labels us as human.**

God knew this would happen to your marriage yet still made you the mom of your kids. You are the only one, the best one, for the job of raising your children. You are the one God called to guide them through this difficult season and love them with your whole heart, even on the hardest of days. God doesn't expect perfection from you, so don't expect it from yourself.

There will be countless opportunities in the coming months and years for you to doubt your ability as a mom. Don't fall into that trap. Capture negative thoughts, and refuse to listen when the enemy whispers lies of failure and inadequacy.

You've got this, mama. You are enough, and God is enough to fill in the gaps. Don't let the emotion of inadequacy or guilt keep you from being the beautiful, wonderful, capable, and fully qualified mom God designed you to be. Don't let criticism from a spouse or the struggle of co-parenting steal the joy of being the mom your kids adore and desperately need. Have confidence in the abilities God gave you and in yourself, and remember to lean into Him on the toughest days of parenting. Simply do your best and trust God with the rest.

Love Yourself

You are still as valuable today as the day God carefully formed you in the womb. But this path we are on as women walking through separation and divorce tempts us to think the polar opposite. Your mind might be weighed down by words that do not imply value, such as: *Disposable. Tossed aside. Replaceable. Unwanted. Unloved. Unvalued. Unimportant.*

These words describe how I felt for so long—for years during my marriage and even more so after it ended. As much as I hope you don't feel and think the same way, you likely do because it's impossible to escape the pull of self-condemnation when someone we loved implies we don't matter. The cavernous levels of insecurities that branch out of such deep rejection are a bottomless pit.

If you google the term *self-love*, you'll find a lot of differing opinions on the subject, some saying we should love ourselves and some saying it's vain and worldly. But how can we love others if we don't love ourselves? Jesus told a religious leader that the second most important commandment is "Love your neighbor as yourself" (Mark 12:31). This simple rule was important enough to be included eight times in the Bible.

With that in mind, think about how you treat yourself. Do you love yourself as much as you love your neighbor? Are the words you say to yourself loving, kind, fair, uplifting, complimentary? Or are they negative, harsh, critical, discouraging, and insulting? Are the thoughts you think about yourself—or the things you say to yourself when you look in the mirror—composed of words you would ever say to someone else? Even your worst enemy? If not, my friend, this is the perfect place to jump-start your journey to recovery. We tend to be willing to extend grace, love, and compassion to others, forgive their mistakes, overlook their shortcomings, and breathe life into them, but we rarely do that for ourselves. Yet we are so worth it, and the fact is, we can't give others our best if we are not at our best. We all need to learn to love ourselves again. But how do we do that?

> God doesn't expect perfection from you, so don't expect it from yourself.

First, get to know yourself again. Take out a notepad and a pen, snuggle up in a comfy chair, and think hard about the gifts and talents you were blessed with. Write them down one by one. Think about your hobbies (now or in earlier days), your accomplishments, the things you are most proud of, and the goals you've met. Think about how much you do for your children and others and the love and blessings you bring to their lives. Consider all the good things that make you special. In other words, have a private brag session on little ole you. You don't have to share it with anyone, so let yourself see yourself as God sees you.

Second, practice transforming your thoughts every day. For example, each time you think *I'm not good enough for anyone*, remind yourself how adored you are by your heavenly Father and how many precious people in your life *do* think you're enough. Each time you think *I'm a terrible mom*, tell yourself you are not perfect but God decided you were the perfect mom for your kids and you're doing the best you can. Each time you think *I can't get through this problem* or *I can't take another day*, remind yourself all things are possible with Christ. Turn every negative into a positive, and you'll be amazed how your attitude and perspective begin to transform.

Third, be kind to yourself. You may not like some things about yourself, or you may have made mistakes, but every self-condemning thought affects who you are today and how you live. Each one pollutes your view of yourself and damages your self-esteem and self-worth.

Fourth, protect your own heart while it's mending. You are in a fragile place, and it may take every ounce of willpower you can muster to get through each day and avoid falling apart. So if there are people in your life who love you deeply but are making this journey even harder, don't be afraid to set some boundaries. At a minimum, let them know how they are hurting instead of helping. It is important to always love others and be kind, especially to those who love us and just want to help. But remember, it's also okay to limit time with people whose attempts to help are emotionally draining or hurtful.

There will also likely be people who make wrong assumptions or judgments about you or your situation. Don't worry about them. I imagine you already have enough real problems to deal with without letting someone else's words or opinions dictate your happiness. Your heart deserves some tender loving care right now.

Breathe life into yourself today. Just as you would put on your oxygen mask before aiding others if you were on an airplane in distress, this is the time to start putting yourself first. You can't care for others if you don't take care of yourself first. And you are worth it.

Fifth, spend time in prayer. Thank God for how He made you and who He created you to be. Imagine yourself smiling and happy again, not because life is perfect or you're perfect but because God did not make a mistake when He designed you. As we're told in Psalm 139:13–14, "You made all the delicate, inner parts of my body and knit me together in my mother's womb. Thank you for making me so wonderfully complex! Your workmanship is marvelous—how well I know it."

Open your eyes, and let yourself see the precious *you* God created, not the *you* who's been defining herself by the hurtful actions or words of someone else. Not the *you* defined and scarlet-lettered by mistakes, sin, or regrets. Not the *you* who feels broken and tossed aside. Then accept that person once and for all and love her—not in vanity but with humility. Accept that you are imperfect and life dealt you a hard blow, but believe that your value in God's eyes never changes.

Scripture includes so many passages about God's love for us, but one verse sums it all up: "This is how God loved the world: He gave his one and only Son, so that everyone who believes in him will not perish but have eternal life" (John 3:16). We were valuable enough for Jesus to die for, with no strings attached. Let's not ever take that truth for granted or allow the hardships of life, our own imperfections and sins, or the treatment of others to cause us to forget the depth of our value.

> *You've got this, mama. You are enough, and God is enough to fill in the gaps.*

Last, be yourself. You are embarking on a whole new season of life. Why not determine to love yourself in this season? I promise it will take less energy to love yourself than it will to despise yourself!

Maybe you feel like you've lost yourself over the years. Maybe you can hardly remember the pre-wedding *you* and you wonder whether you can ever get that girl back. Repeat after me right now: *Yes, I can!* If you can't find any reason to love yourself, think about it this way. You can't ever feel truly happy until you make peace with who you are. This is why loving yourself is so crucial.

Through faith and perseverance, even if you're not typically one to pat yourself on the back for accomplishments or acknowledge your good traits, you can do this. You can become the best *you* ever—starting today. Loving yourself is a game changer. Choose to do so.

Love Your God

The second most important commandment is to love yourself, but the first is to love your God. Jesus said, "The most important commandment is this: 'Listen, O Israel! The LORD our God is the one and only LORD. And you must love the LORD your God with all your heart, all your soul, all your mind, and all your strength" (Mark 12:29–30). Loving God with your whole heart, soul, and mind can be challenging when life is hard and you feel forgotten.

It's easy to have a good attitude and love God when life is going smoothly. When your marriage is happy. When your spouse is faithful. When your kids excel and behave. When family life is peaceful. When your dreams come true. But it's also easy to stop loving God and develop a toxic, negative attitude when it all goes south. When your prayers seem to go unanswered, your problems are mounting, and nothing good seems to be happening in your life.

Gracious, it's certainly not easy to trust God during the toughest of times, much less follow His principles for life when we feel like He's not intervening in our situation. When He seems so distant that we can't hear His voice anymore. However, pulling away from God or turning our backs on Him is the absolute worst thing we can do, and we suffer so many negative consequences if we do.

There is nothing more important than continuing to love God through our pain and letting Him love us, guide us, and hold us up when we can't take another step. It's imperative to believe He is our friend walking beside us on this journey.

Months after my husband left, I had an incredible, life-changing dream that reminded me God was with me. I wanted to remember it, so I recorded it in my journal:

I woke up this morning at 7:30 a.m. and got SO excited that I slept all night for the first time in months without waking. And I had this weird dream all night that I was in Israel, with Jesus, and we were walking around and talking, and He was so sweet and gentle and comforting. I don't remember what He was talking about, or any profound instruction or wisdom. I don't remember being able to see His face fully, but it was Him. And I knew it. It seemed to go on for hours. Just doing life, walking calmly through the day, with Jesus. But I had this unusual happy feeling when I woke up. It was weird. But it was wonderful. I think Jesus gave me that dream to let me know He is with me, right beside me, walking through every step of life. My invisible companion, but present and close by nonetheless.

Close your eyes and imagine this was your dream. Picture Jesus beside you, your companion. Imagine yourself holding hands with Him as He smiles at you, walking through the streets, and taking in the sights, sounds, and scents of your surroundings. Let your ears hear His soft voice speaking words of comfort and love that calm your soul. Let His presence lull you into a peaceful state. Think about how full your heart would be in that moment, and let that feeling sink deep into your soul. Hang on to that feeling.

His Promises Will Get You Through

Here are seven biblical promises to help you remember that although we all fall short of perfection, God never does. He provides everything we need to be the greatest version of ourselves and enjoy the life He is allowing us to live. You might want to review these on those days when you have a mom meltdown or feel down about yourself, your life, or your ability to take one more breath.

Remember …

Love conquers all. Love your children, love yourself, and love your God. "Love never gives up, never loses faith, is always hopeful, and endures through every circumstance" (1 Cor. 13:7).

God is your helper. You may be a single parent now and struggling as a newly single person, but your heavenly Father is still by your side. He will get you through those days when you feel you can't take another step. "He gives power to the weak and strength to the powerless" (Isa. 40:29).

God sees and cares. He knows what you're going through, and He is arranging the details of your life to rescue you from your troubles and provide for your needs. "The eyes of the LORD watch over those who do right; his ears are open to their cries for help.... The LORD hears his people when they call to him for help. He rescues them from all their troubles" (Ps. 34:15, 17).

God is always with you. And He always will be. He is as close as you allow Him to be. "The LORD is close to the brokenhearted; he rescues those whose spirits are crushed" (Ps. 34:18).

You are enough. On those days when you feel you aren't, depend on Him to fill in the gaps and give you strength. "My grace is sufficient for you, for my power is made perfect in weakness" (2 Cor. 12:9 ESV).

Gratitude is a game changer. Every day may not be a good day, but every day you can rejoice that you were given another day and thank God for the good things in your life and for calling you His. "Be thankful in all circumstances, for this is God's will for you who belong to Christ Jesus" (1 Thess. 5:18).

God is putting the puzzle pieces of your life together, one piece at a time. He promises you a good future. Let your heart and mind rest in that promise. "'I know the plans I have for you,' says the LORD. 'They are plans for good and not for disaster, to give you a future and a hope'" (Jer. 29:11).

Remember … it's going to be okay one day. You are going to be more than okay. Just keep putting one foot in front of the other. Right now, that may be all you can do. Let yourself remember—that is enough.

Happiness Prompters

- Make a list of the simple ways you can be a blessing to your children or others, and create a plan for how to do so.

- Think about goals you have achieved or dreams you have realized, and write down new goals and dreams. Allow yourself to dream big! You can do anything you set your mind to!

Healing Steps

1. Think about what you can do to show your children some extra love today, regardless of their ages. Pay attention to their reactions and expressions, and make note of how every gesture of love, big or small, makes a huge difference in their moods and attitudes.

2. How does knowing that Scripture commands us to love ourselves help you view yourself differently? Consider how your relationships might benefit if you loved yourself as much as you love others. Make a list of ways you can begin to love yourself better.

3. Your invisible companion, Jesus, is walking beside you every day. At least once a day, close your eyes, talk with Him, and let His peace fill your soul.

Caring for You

For the next seven days, read one of the "remember" statements at the end of this chapter and memorize the Scripture associated with it. Repeat this practice each week until these truths are tucked into your heart so deeply that when something happens to threaten your peace and joy, you can recall them to mind quickly.

Chapter 10

It's Time to Turn the Page

One Saturday afternoon a few years ago, I was sitting at home literally bored to tears. I needed a project. Something to occupy not only my hands but also my mind—other than hosting another epic pity party.

Maybe a little purging of clutter would be a good mind-occupying activity. I wandered upstairs to the hot attic, breathed in the musky, damp smell, and began scanning the room. Two cardboard boxes spilling over with forgotten items caught my attention.

I sat down on the bare wood floor and began sifting through the contents. One by one I pulled out items to put in either the "keep for sentimental reasons" pile or the "discard because this never should have been saved in the first place" pile. I smiled as I uncovered photos of my children's cute little faces when they were young, vacation photos that brought back sweet memories, pottery pieces made by tiny hands in elementary school, little handprints painted on construction paper, and more sports team photos than any parent should ever have to purchase.

But when I moved a few other things around, a big white book shifted and peeked out from under the pile. My smile instantly disappeared.

The wedding album.

A book I was once so proud of, replete with pages of once-sweet memories of our special day, now held the power to evoke immense heartache.

I reached over, pulled it out of the box, and blew off a cloud of dust that had settled on it over the years. I opened it up and began flipping through the pages. With each photo of a smiling bride and groom, excited to kick off their life together, my heart sank.

Unfortunately, you and I both know life doesn't always turn out the way we thought it would. Wedding vows aren't always kept, shattering all our little-girl dreams within decades, years, and sometimes only months.

Once again, all alone in a dusty attic, the pain of my failed marriage flew all over me like a swarm of bees. I felt the sting of disappointment and sadness from head to toe as I sat immersed in crushed dreams on the hard attic floor. My mind buzzed with all the what-ifs and if-onlys. Sorrow filled my heart. Tears welled up. Disappointment overload. Again. Cleaning project over.

Disappointment and sorrow are powerful emotions that can keep us stuck in a pattern of focusing on what we lost and mourning dreams that didn't come true. They prevent us from believing God has good plans for us, even greater plans than we had, and stifle our ability to let go of what was supposed to be.

But the truth is, no person or experience has any power over our thoughts or emotions. We can allow disappointment to be a hindrance to our happiness, or we can allow it to help us clarify new goals and move forward. Disappointment will lessen when we change our perception about it. As Lysa TerKeurst shared in her recent book, "These disappointments we all go through are actually divine appointments to see God do a new thing."[1] That couldn't be truer! God is always up to something new. Yet we have to let go of the past in order to embrace the future He is making. The life that awaits us is far more important than the life behind us. It took me a while to understand this, because it was hard to accept what had happened to my family, but when I allowed myself to believe it, life changed.

As I trudged back downstairs from the attic, I took a deep breath and let out a heavy sigh. I was so tired of being stuck on a torn-up page of life. As hard as I knew it would be, I remember thinking how much my heart and mind were finally ready to turn the page. Looking back to that day, I knew I was finally ready for a new story to begin and ready to trust God with whatever the future held. And I did exactly that.

Are you ready for God to start writing your new chapters of life?

> We can allow disappointment to be a hindrance to our happiness, or we can allow it to help us clarify new goals and move forward.

When we stay on the same page of life, stuck in the messy chapters, repeating the same negative thoughts day after day, longing for things that can never be, or reciting our regrets over and over, nothing will ever change. We can't start living out the new story God is writing in our lives until we let go of the old one and accept the life He has us in today.

God is always ahead of us, crafting the events of our story. The story that didn't work out the way we wanted can have a brand-new wonderful ending. A whole new chapter of life awaits. A beautiful and amazing chapter, but we have to turn the page to get there!

The Art of Letting Go

The first way to turn the page of life is to learn how to let go of what's holding your life back. It's hard to let go of anything that is important to us. When it comes to separation and divorce, it's hard to release not only the person we once loved but also the idea of the life we thought we'd have with that person forever.

However, **the only thing harder than letting go is holding on to what can't be.**

Before filing for divorce, I spent months praying for direction and clarity. *Should I let go and move on, God? Should I give up the tiny shred of hope I have for reconciliation? Am I desperately trying to hold this irreparable relationship together simply because I'm terrified of being alone? Should I follow my heart or my head? How do I know what is best for my children? Do I let go of what was and trust You with whatever will be?*

Questions like these plagued my mind on a daily basis, but one evening, I poured them out in prayer like never before. I knew it was time for something to change, so I prayed for the discernment to make a decision with a feeling of peace, void of doubt.

The next morning, as I read my daily devotion, my heart began to race. It felt as if I was finally hearing the voice of God speaking directly to the questions I had been moaning to Him for months and had uttered with humble fervency just the night before. I don't believe in coincidences—only God-incidences—and this was certainly one.

> Strive to trust Me in more and more areas of your life.... *Don't waste energy regretting the way things are or thinking about what might have been. Start at the present moment—accepting things exactly as they are—and search for My way in the midst of those circumstances.*
>
> Trust is like a staff you can lean on as you journey uphill with Me. If you are trusting in Me consistently, the staff will bear as much of your weight as needed. *Lean on, trust, and be confident in Me with all your heart and mind.* Psalm 52:8[2]

I shared in an earlier chapter that before filing for divorce, I felt God had released me to make that decision. This is that moment when a sense of peace filled me, knowing God had heard my prayers. I finally knew and believed He would carry me in my weakest moments of indecision even when I was doubting His sovereignty and fed up with the circumstances I was facing. I felt in my spirit this was His way of telling me I could trust Him, let go of the past, and move forward in faith. I could live in peace, no matter what happened and even if I was single, because I wasn't carrying the weight of the world all alone.

I never wanted to be divorced, I didn't want to have a broken family, and I certainly didn't want my children to be from a broken home. The words *broken* and *broken family* haunted my mind for many months until I shared my feelings with my sweet friend Leah. She lovingly said, "Tracie, just because your marriage didn't work doesn't mean you are a broken person, and your home is not broken either. When people pass away and go to heaven, for example, their family isn't broken; it's just different. It is missing a person who used to be there, but they are still a whole wonderful family." Her words helped me stop obsessing over feeling and looking broken and getting hung up on cultural clichés. She helped me accept that I could be whole and healed while knowing the change had to begin within me.

I had no doubt my situation broke my heavenly Father's heart, for me, my husband, and my children, because He loves us all. But I also had no doubt He loved me unconditionally and would be by my side every single day.

After reading this devotion, I was finally convinced God was giving me permission to let go. To turn the page. To be brave and move forward. To face single life with courage. To trust Him with all things and let Him breathe fresh hope into my next season of life. To feel and live unbroken.

Letting go is necessary in order to make strides forward in the newness of our lives. It's not easy, but there are practical things we can do to help us make progress one day at a time.

> *The only thing harder than letting go is holding on to what can't be.*

In her book *Runaway Husbands*, Vikki Stark wrote about a woman named Stacey who adopted a simple personal mantra to help her let go of the past and embrace the present after she went through her divorce. Stacey said, "I wrote LET IT GO on index cards and placed them everywhere I was likely to look. I put one on my bathroom mirror. I put one on my nightstand. I put one on the fridge door. I taped one to the dashboard of my car." She went on to say she put one on her desk, in her lesson plan book, and in her purse—and even whispered "Let it go" to herself in the dark as she went to sleep each night. She would repeat it over and over throughout her days. Stacey said, "That constant reaffirmation of doing the only thing I really could do was a great help to me."[3] Even if all you can muster the energy for is to whisper "Let it go" over and over, then do it, and consider that a valuable step forward.

You could also write down the positives that have transpired since the end of your marriage. Although it might be hard to think of some at first, they do exist! For example, maybe you've learned to be more independent and stand on your own two feet. Perhaps you're enjoying your new freedom; you no longer have to live in an abusive or controlling or loveless relationship; you have new hopes and dreams which you now feel free to pursue.

Either of these things may be helpful for you, but if not, contemplate other ways you could consistently remind yourself of your need to let it go, let him go, let the visions you had of the future go, let the hurt go, let the unforgiveness go. Whatever is holding you back from moving forward in mind, spirit, and body, let it go and grab hold of the good things trying to grow roots.

Letting go allows you to start living life differently and experience true healing and happiness. It can also be the beginning of breaking free from pain because when you release the past, you also release yourself to start a happy, hope-filled life.

And how about if you begin looking at your divorce with a new perspective? I was blown away by the life-changing perspective God gave Malinda, which helped her let go and begin turning her life around.

In both of her failed marriages, Malinda felt replaceable, disposable, disappointed. All these feelings strangled her self-worth and caused her to act out of character, but she continued participating in a Bible study at her church. Malinda shared with me, "Through studying the story of Esther, I learned I wasn't what I thought. I wasn't replaced but released. Released from feeling unworthy, unloved, disregarded, disrespected, and not valued for the person and woman I am in Christ. I've become reliant on my worth in Christ and not my relationships. I am an awesome spirit being of magnificent worth as a person because Christ died for me."

Sometimes disappointment can change when our perception changes. Malinda suggested, "Could it be, as difficult and painful as it was, that God was releasing you from the pain you were living in and the loveless future that lay ahead, and rejection was simply the means to make that happen? Could it be He was protecting you from harm down the road?" Let your mind ponder that. You are released. Even if it's not what you would have chosen, you are now free to live your life to the fullest.

As I let her words sink in, I thought, *As sad as I am that my marriage didn't last forever and as sad as I am for my children that they no* longer have their father in their lives, I believe God saw the years of pain and silent suffering I had endured and this was His way of protecting all of us. He released me from what couldn't be. He released me from being stuck in a painful situation I had no control over so I could begin anew and pursue happiness. He released me to be able to see myself through His eyes instead of my own or someone else's. I was released to begin believing life could be wonderful again and believing in myself. I was released to be able to begin to believe I am enough.

> Letting go allows you to start living life differently and experience true healing and happiness.

Diana also discovered the joy of being *released*. After twenty-five years of marriage, Diana was facing divorce due to her husband's infidelity. God led her to attend DivorceCare classes at her church, which helped her begin to heal and eventually let go of what couldn't be and embrace her new life. In doing that, she felt empowered and excited and began to see her life blossom into something more wonderful than she ever could have imagined. She said, "My grown children are married and have given me seven wonderful grandchildren. I'm sixty-seven, happily single, and relocated to live my fantasy island life on tropical Maui, Hawaii. I own a condo with an ocean view and work full time as an accountant for a vacation rental resort complex on the beach! Looking back, I know God meant my life to be a witness of surviving and thriving!"

Don't you love that? Obviously, we can't all move to Hawaii (although that would be nice!), but we can all thrive in this next chapter of life in our own ways and wherever we are. Don't overthink it; just choose to be happy no matter what.

Life is what we make of it. Let's make the most.

Whether you're at rock bottom lying on the cold kitchen floor or you're months or years into dealing with the loss and feeling like you're going to survive after all, you have the power to decide if you're going to be happy or unhappy every single day. In fact, if you're at rock bottom, that is actually the perfect place to begin starting over. But whether you're at the bottom of the pit or slowly making your way out, you can choose to adopt a positive outlook on life.

Reclaim Your Happiness

If we truly want to escape the rut of sadness and hopelessness and to heal and move forward, it is imperative we take an active role in rebuilding our lives and reclaiming our happiness, not just sit and wait for it to happen or merely hope it will. The truth is, **your happiness is up to you.** I've already shared lots of practical tips for how to start moving forward, but as this book comes to a close, I want to share a few more ideas for how you can take an active role in turning your life around and starting anew.

Find a Purpose

Find something of meaning to focus on—something you are passionate about that makes you feel good while taking your mind off your troubles. Finding a purpose can help you move forward and pursue happiness successfully.

As single moms, raising our kids gives us purpose. As employees, doing our jobs to the best of our ability gives us purpose. These things can bring happiness and satisfaction. But when we pursue individual purpose for our lives, a calling we are passionate about that has a positive impact on the lives of others, true happiness can begin to rise from the depths of your heart.

Writing about my journey in the hopes of helping other women is my passion and also my purpose. It gives me something positive to focus on. Knowing God has placed this call on my life compels me to keep pursuing it, even when I don't feel like it and even when I'd rather keep my dirty laundry to myself. Seeing God use our pain for a purpose is a major salve for the wounds of our hearts.

The women who have shared their stories in this book also discovered the benefits of living with purpose. Malinda's passion is helping others in any way she can, including making crafts to sell and giving a portion of what she earns to two churches in her town. Kristen feels called to share her story with others and wants to one day lead a support group for women who are hurting. Holly is passionate about encouraging women to know who they are in Christ and to see value in themselves. Her passion turned into a "craft therapy" business. She teaches women paper crafting (card making, scrapbooking, etc.), which gives them an outlet to be a blessing to others. She also likes to write and encourage others in their faith journeys and has become a business coach for women who want to use their passions to create a business. Denise enjoys mentoring people going through difficult times in their marriages and letting them know they do not need to suffer alone.

Think about the gifts and talents you are blessed with and the things you enjoy doing, and consider how you could use those to bring glory to God. I wrote more about turning your pain into purpose in my book *Your Life Still Counts: How God Uses Your Past to Create a Beautiful Future.*

Do Something You've Always Wanted to Do

Another way to kick-start happiness is to do something you weren't able to do before your divorce. Can you find happiness from buying new kitchen utensils? That's exactly what Meagan did! Her husband was controlling and always made her get by with what she had, so she felt a sense of freedom when she decided to replace the old utensils in her kitchen with brand-new ones. Cyndi's husband was controlling as well, but after he left, she went out and bought a new bedspread—with flowers on it! It lifts her spirits each time she walks into her bedroom.

As silly as these small things may sound, doing little acts of independence made these women feel liberated and gave them a sense of happiness again—and isn't that what matters? These are great reminders that we are the only ones who can define what happiness is to us. If you need something to smile about, make it happen!

Take Control of What You Can

Figure out what you do have control over, and do something empowering. Taking control of my finances and my home after my ex left helped me feel more in control and helped me build confidence. Admittedly, I spent months in a panic, trying to get my head around it all, but I made progress, one issue and anxiety attack at a time.

I canceled certain accounts and services and signed up for less-expensive ones. I had a security system installed, which made me feel safer in my own home. I purchased a handgun and took a class to earn my concealed carry permit. I painted and redecorated a spare room in my house, transforming it into a perfectly cozy, girly-girl office. I bought a dainty comforter for my bed, and my mom sewed pastel blue curtains to match. I swapped out the photos on the walls of my home for ones of just the kids, rather than entire family photos that were constant reminders of who was missing from our lives. I couldn't control everything, but what I could control, I did.

Find a Counselor

We all like to think we can handle life on our own, but sometimes we simply can't. There is no shame in seeking counseling to help us work through life's struggles. I've met with several counselors over the years, and they have helped so much with processing my thoughts, emotions, and fears and managing my PTSD symptoms. I even attended a few DivorceCare classes, which helped me feel less alone in my feelings. Natalie also shared that after her husband refused to go to counseling and refused to get divorced, she began to go to counseling herself, and it made all the difference in the world. She gained the strength to do what she needed to do and start her own healing process. Sometimes the simple act of talking things out with someone can be life changing.

Start a Habit of Journaling

My digital journal has become a treasure, helping me remember how far I have come and how God has been at work in my life. Natalie also took up journaling about her experience because she realized how hard it was to get all her thoughts expressed verbally. She began to write out her questions to God and to look for answers in His Word. When she saw it all written out in black and white, everything that had happened and what she needed to do became much clearer. She eventually grew to believe she had done all she could do and that she was free to let go of her marriage and move on. Holly began journaling and keeping track of her blessings so she would always be aware of what God was doing in her life. When bad days came, her journal reminded her of God's faithfulness.

Journaling was an outlet for me as well as a habit I took seriously. Even though looking back at my journal entries today often serves as a reminder of all the pain I went through, it also reminds me how much I've overcome and achieved and how far God has brought me.

Find an Accountability Partner

When Holly finally decided to let go of the past, she took several tangible steps to make her decision real. She cleaned her house and got rid of reminders of trauma that hindered her healing. She then told trusted friends about her decisions and asked them to be her accountability partners when she was tempted to look back.

Sue sold things her ex-husband left behind—the fewer reminders the better. She cooked meals she loved and began making more decisions on her own. Her advice is excellent: "There is something to be said for taking one step each day." This made me recall a popular old Chinese saying: "The journey of a thousand miles begins with a single step." This journey may seem long. You may not see the end right now. But every baby step in the direction of happiness and healing gets you a little closer to where you really want to be.

Do What You Love

What do you love doing? What excites you and makes you want to hop out of bed? Where does your sense of accomplishment come from? What are you passionate about? Let each thing you do make you feel good about yourself and your contributions to others. Focus on the joy you receive from what you're doing today, and live fully in the moment.

Let Yourself Dream

Where do you want to see yourself in a year, five years, or ten years? Is what you're doing today setting you up for where you want to be then? Have you allowed yourself time to dream about what you want your future to look like rather than just worry about how it might turn out? Giving yourself permission to dream is a powerful way to propel yourself forward with optimism and renewed hope. We all need something to look forward to, something fun and uplifting to focus on. Blow the dust off those dreams you once had, or think of new ones that have been in the back of your mind lately, and start making a solid plan for making them a reality.

> *Giving yourself permission to dream is a powerful way to propel yourself forward.*

Do not be afraid to dream big! All things are possible with God, and He knows the desires of our hearts. In the words of Cinderella, a dream is a wish your heart makes.[4] But a dream will remain merely a wish until we start putting action steps into place. So once you've got your dreams thought out, use some of the goal-setting tips I shared in chapter 5 to begin formulating a plan to make them happen. Set one or more long-term goals for your dreams (even lofty, seemingly impossible goals!), and then write out all the small subgoals it will take to achieve the larger vision. In other words, map out all the little steps needed to help you achieve your desired result. For each small goal you reach, reward yourself! After a while your small goals will snowball and get you closer and closer to where you want to be. Before you know it, your dreams will stop being wishes and start coming true!

Create a Vision Board

To put a fun spin on goal setting and dreaming, create a vision board—a sacred space that displays your goals. A vision board can bring your dreams to life and also serve as a daily reminder of your goals to help you stay motivated. Cut out photos from magazines of things that inspire you, places you want to go, and personal goals you want to achieve. Include photos of women smiling, single women and moms thriving. Keep in mind your vision should focus on how you want to feel, not only what you want to have or do.

Look for Ways God Has Already Been at Work

Sometimes we may miss the things God is doing in our lives because we are so focused on what we think He isn't doing or the problems He hasn't fixed yet. At times we may not even realize we are walking through doors we prayed He would open, reaping prayed-for blessings. Especially on days when you're feeling discouraged, take time to look around and see where God has been at work. Look back at your journal if you keep one, and read the prayers that once dripped off your pen as quickly as the tears from your eyes. I venture to guess you will be able to see evidence that you are living in the midst of the answer to one of your forgotten prayers.

Keep an Open Mind

Last, embrace your new life with an open mind, open heart, and open hands. Receive all the newness God has for you, and make sure your mind-set is positive and hopeful, not negative and hopeless.

At some point we all have to stop dwelling on the past and live in the present. We have to shift our focus to good things instead of bad. We have to realize when it's time to let go of the old and embrace the new.

Today is where life is happening, not last week, last month, or last year. We can't move forward if we keep looking at what's behind us. Don't let the past steal your future. The only time you should be looking back is to see just how far you've come.

You may never be happy that divorce is part of your story. Even if you are happy and it was something you knew was best for you, part of you may sometimes wish things could have turned out differently. But we can't give up just because we have one bad chapter in life. There are many more chapters ahead! The time will come when you begin to accept your new normal and your heart will be ready. You will start feeling happy again and develop a desire to meet new people, start dating, move into a new home, get a new job, enjoy being single and independent, and truly begin to move on with your life. That may seem impossible right now, but I promise you, it will happen.

Embracing the New

Nobody likes change, but change is a part of life. In the months following a divorce, so many challenges lurk around every corner. Everything looks and feels different. Unfamiliar. Foreign. New—and not a good type of new. It's easy to sink under the weight of toxic emotions and worries. But new is not always bad—in fact, God promised us in Scripture that new is good.

Isaiah 43:18 says, "Forget all that—it is nothing compared to what I am going to do." In this chapter, God predicted the deliverance of Israel from Babylon and spoke to the Israelites who would be stuck in the past, remembering the miracles God had done yet fearing the freedom they now lived in. In verse 19, we see God telling them *why* to stop looking back: "For I am about to do something new. See, I have already begun! Do you not see it?"

Here God encouraged them to let go of the old and embrace the new, even though this new seemed scary. He wanted them to open their eyes to see that He was still at work and still sovereign. By keeping their eyes focused on the past, they were blinded to the new good things He was doing. God perceived this habit was standing in the way of their embracing the new with a positive, hopeful mind-set—even if they had no idea what the new was going to look like.

Next, God tried to ease their minds by reminding them what the new actually was: "I will make a pathway through the wilderness. I will create rivers in the dry wasteland" (v. 19b). You see, hundreds of miles of rough terrain and deserts stretched ahead of the Israelites in their journey out of captivity in Babylon. God reminded them that not only had He performed miracles in the past but He also already had plans for more wondrous things for them in the future. They simply needed to step into the unfamiliar, hard territory with faith and healed hearts instead of worry and fear.

Let these verses be your permission to move forward, and trust that God has a great plan for you. A lot of things seem out of our control when we go through trauma, but we can control our vision of the future. We can't change our circumstances, but we can change our thoughts about them.

> *Letting go of the old frees up our hearts to embrace God's new.*

Our individual seasons of "new" likely look quite different for each of us, since we are in different seasons of life with different circumstances, challenges, and concerns. But regardless of the new that lies before us, how we choose to look at those seasons of newness will determine whether we walk through them with peace, hope, and joy or with heartache, anxiety, and fear.

When we choose to believe God's new is always good—even if we didn't ask for it, want it, understand it, or like it—we can step into this new season with courage, a positive attitude, and lots of hope. Letting go of the old frees up our hearts to embrace God's new.

I started this chapter by sharing about the time I needed a project to occupy my mind. Something to distract me and keep me busy for a while. I've taken on a lot of new projects over the years for that reason and to help me embrace my season of newness. But the most important lesson I've learned is this: **the best project we can ever work on is ourselves**.

All the tips and suggestions I've shared in this book are ways you can build yourself up again—improve yourself, your confidence, and your life overall. Although my life is not void of problems, I am past surviving and into thriving. I actually love my life and all the people in it. My children are doing wonderfully, and I keep my family close. I have many treasured friends and an active social life. I enjoy what I do for a living. I spend time doing things I love and have picked up new hobbies. I've managed to live comfortably on my own and stay afloat financially. I've learned to appreciate the little things in life and be content with what I have. Life is not perfect, but it is good. Sometimes I even think, *I made it! Look what God has done!* And a little smile creeps across my face and also my heart.

You too will survive, and you will thrive. But change can only happen when we are truly ready to make a change. No pages in a book or advice from a friend will make it happen for you. Only you are in charge of changing the way you've been living and thinking, and only you can embrace the life God has planned for you with an open mind. You are in control of your happiness, my friend.

Even if you and I aren't right where we want to be just yet, at least we're not where we used to be. Your present reality does not define your whole life. Time passes more quickly than we realize, and before you know it, one day you will wake up and a smile will creep across your face and heart too. Will you let yourself believe that?

Never consider yourself broken again, because you are a whole, beautiful being God created regardless of what has happened in your past. Psalm 118:13 says, "I was pushed hard, so that I was falling, but the LORD helped me" (ESV). You have been pushed to the breaking point and probably fallen hard but, oh, sweet friend, God is mending the cracks in your heart, filling the voids in your spirit, and making all the pieces of your life new.

This is your life. Nobody else's. It's yours. And it's the only one you get. Permit yourself to live your life to the fullest. Let go of the old, get excited about the new, and hold on tight because the ride is amazing. It may be bumpy at times, but it's going to take your breath away.

God is on the cusp of writing an incredible new ending to your story. A beautiful story. Turn the page and let Him begin.

Happiness Prompters

- Think of every possible way to treat yourself. Over the next few weeks, try to make each of these things happen.
- Look up a new recipe and make it, even if you're only cooking for one. I find cooking and baking to be relaxing and a great mood booster, but if that's not for you, seek out a great new restaurant in town and order something unique from the menu!
- What creative activities do you find energizing and affirming? Go ahead and do them, even if you think you're not great or have it perfected! Just let yourself have fun.

Healing Steps

1. In your journal, write down the benefits that have come from your separation or divorce. How are you better off or happier now than when you were married? In what ways have you grown? What life lessons have you learned that will be helpful down the road?

2. Write out what God may have released you from by allowing your marriage to end. How are you possibly better off by going through this situation?

3. Make a list of things you need to let go of in order to move forward. Maybe it's a person, a lifestyle, a financial status, your reputation, or a dream. Maybe emotions or a habit of doom-and-gloom thinking are holding your heart hostage. Whatever is holding you back from moving forward in faith with a smile on your face and in your heart, let it go.

4. Embrace your singleness today, sweet friend! Live life to the fullest!

Caring for You

True happiness may still seem elusive right now, but trust that one thing will happen every day to bring joy to your heart, and be on the lookout for it. Create a happiness jar to keep track of happy moments. Each day write down on a little piece of paper something good that happened. A blessing you felt thankful for, whether big or small—one you want to remember. One year later, you'll have an entire jar of happy moments to help you get excited about the new year!

Whenever you're doubting God is at work or you're having a really bad day, pull out your happy memories and read through them. Let them lift your spirits as you're reminded of God's faithfulness.

Notes

Chapter 1: When Your World Is Shattered

1. William Cowper, "Charity," in *Poems*, 3rd ed. (Glasgow: D. MacVean, 1830), 95.

2. Christina Gregory, "The Five Stages of Grief: An Examination of the Kubler-Ross Model," PsyCom, last modified June 25, 2020, www.psycom.net/depression.central .grief.html. The descriptions of the five stages of grief included under each heading are drawn from this source.

3. Gregory, "Five Stages of Grief."

4. Sarah Young, *Jesus Calling: Enjoying Peace in His Presence* (Nashville: Thomas Nelson, 2004), July 16.

Chapter 3: Your Fears Are No Match for God

1. Judith Orloff, "The Health Benefits of Tears," *Psychology Today*, July 27, 2010, www.psychologytoday.com/us/blog/emotional-freedom/201007/ the-health-benefits-tears.

2. Sarah Young, *Jesus Calling: Enjoying Peace in His Presence* (Nashville: Thomas Nelson, 2004), December 28.

3. Max Lucado, *Jesus: The God Who Knows Your Name* (Nashville: Nelson Books, 2020), 108.

Chapter 4: Overcoming Loneliness

1. Lynn Darling, "Is There a Medical Cure for Loneliness?," AARP, December 11, 2019, www.aarp.org/home-family/friends-family/info-2019/medical-cure-for -loneliness.html.

2. Louise Hawkley, quoted in Darling, "Is There a Medical Cure for Loneliness?"

3. Lynda Flowers et al., "Medicare Spends More on Socially Isolated Older Adults," AARP Public Policy Institute, November 2017, www.aarp.org/content/dam/aarp/ppi/2017/10/medicare-spends-more-on-socially-isolated-older-adults.pdf.

4. Aric Jenkins, "Study Finds That Half of Americans—Especially Young People—Feel Lonely," *Fortune*, May 1, 2018, https://fortune.com/2018/05/01/americans-lonely-cigna-study.

5. Darling, "Is There a Medical Cure for Loneliness?"

6. *Merriam-Webster*, s.v. "isolation," accessed August 5, 2020, www.merriam-webster.com/dictionary/isolation.

7. Vikki Stark, *Runaway Husbands: The Abandoned Wife's Guide to Recovery and Renewal* (Montreal: Green Light Press, 2010), 35.

Chapter 5: Making the Most of Your Singleness

1. Dr. Seuss, *Oh, the Places You'll Go!* (New York: Random House Children's Books, 1988).

Chapter 6: Breaking the Power of Shame

1. Darlene Lancer, "Emotions after Divorce," WomansDivorce.com, December 18, 2018, www.womansdivorce.com/emotions-after-divorce.html.

Chapter 7: Releasing the Burden of Guilt

1. Karen Covy, "Is Divorce Guilt Getting You Down?," HuffPost, November 2, 2015, www.huffpost.com/entry/is-divorce-guilt-getting-you-down_b_8433984.

2. Lysa TerKeurst, *It's Not Supposed to Be This Way: Finding Unexpected Strength When Disappointments Leave You Shattered* (Nashville: Nelson Books, 2018), 150.

3. Shawn Achor, *The Happiness Advantage: The Seven Principles of Positive Psychology That Fuel Success and Performance at Work* (New York: Crown Business, 2010), 53–54.

Chapter 8: Girl, You Are Not Crazy

1. Támara Hill, "Grief and Trauma: 5 Stages to Overcome," PsychCentral, September 26, 2018, https://blogs.psychcentral.com/caregivers/2018/09/grief-trauma-5-stages-to-overcome/.

2. "Post-Traumatic Stress Disorder," National Institute of Mental Health, last modified May 2019, www.nimh.nih.gov/health/topics/post-traumatic-stress-disorder-ptsd/index.shtml.

3. Allison Abrams, "Post-Divorce Trauma and PTSD," Verywell Mind, last modified March 22, 2020, www.verywellmind.com/post-divorce-trauma-4583824.

4. Toni Coleman, quoted in Abrams, "Post-Divorce Trauma and PTSD."

5. James S. Gordon, quoted in Stephanie Eckelkamp, "Can Trauma Really Be 'Stored' in the Body?," Mindbodygreen, October 9, 2019, www.mindbodygreen .com/articles/can-trauma-be-stored-in-body.

6. Shaili Jain, quoted in Eckelkamp, "Can Trauma Really Be 'Stored' in the Body?"

7. Karen Covy, "Post Traumatic Growth: The Ultimate Way to Recover from Divorce," Karen Covy, August 10, 2017, https://karencovy.com/post-traumatic -growth-recover-from-divorce.

8. Olympia LePoint, "Triabrain Emotions," Answers Unleashed, accessed September 9, 2020, https://answersunleashed.com/project/episode-11-regaining -mental-peace-trauma/.

9. Debbie McGauran, "Distressing Facts on Emotional Trauma," ActiveBeat, January 25, 2016, www.activebeat.com/your-health/8-distressing-facts-on -emotional-trauma.

10. Wikipedia, s.v. "post-traumatic growth," last modified July 22, 2020, https://en.wikipedia.org/wiki/Posttraumatic_growth.

11. Katie Hanson, "What Is PTG: The Science of Post-Traumatic Growth," PositivePsychology.org.uk, January 16, 2010, http://positivepsychology.org.uk /post-traumatic-growth; Covy, "Post Traumatic Growth."

Chapter 10: It's Time to Turn the Page

1. Lysa TerKeurst, *It's Not Supposed to Be This Way: Finding Unexpected Strength When Disappointments Leave You Shattered* (Nashville: Nelson Books, 2018), 186.

2. Sarah Young, *Jesus Calling: Enjoying Peace in His Presence* (Nashville: Thomas Nelson, 2004), January 22, emphasis added to paragraph 1.

3. Vikki Stark, *Runaway Husbands: The Abandoned Wife's Guide to Recovery and Renewal* (Montreal: Green Light Press, 2010), 89.

4. Ilene Woods, vocalist, "A Dream Is a Wish Your Heart Makes," by Mack David, Jerry Livingston, and Al Hoffman, recorded October 26, 1949, with Harold Mooney on *Cinderella*, RCA Victor Records 31-0014B.

Also by Tracie Miles

Love Life Again: Finding Joy When Life Is Hard

Unsinkable Faith: God-Filled Strategies to Transform the Way You Think, Feel, and Live

Stressed-Less Living: Finding God's Peace in Your Chaotic World

Your Life Still Counts: How God Uses Your Past to Create a Beautiful Future

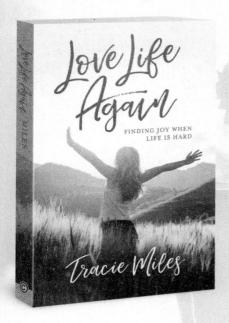

DON'T *let the* STORMS *of* LIFE *pull you* UNDER.

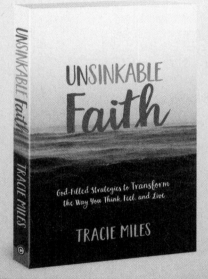

When life's storms beat us down with negativity, it's sometimes hard to resurface. *Unsinkable Faith* shares real-life stories and practical applications of God's truths to remind us that we can stay afloat. When we intentionally choose a life of optimism, our faith and hope become unsinkable, and so do we.

Available in print and digital wherever Christian books are sold

DAVID C COOK

transforming lives together.